Louis Delpla

History of the Sodalities of the Blessed Virgin Mary

a memorial of the tercentenary jubilee. 1584-1884

Louis Delpia

History of the Sodalities of the Blessed Virgin Mary
a memorial of the tercentenary jubilee. 1584-1884

ISBN/EAN: 9783337300302

Printed in Europe, USA, Canada, Australia, Japan

Cover: Foto ©Lupo / pixelio.de

More available books at **www.hansebooks.com**

Copyright
BY THOMAS B. NOONAN & CO.
1884

ELECTROTYPED
BY C. J. PETERS AND SON, BOSTON

TO THE BRETHREN
OF OUR LADY'S SODALITY
IN THE UNITED STATES,
ALREADY NUMEROUS, FERVENT, AND ORGANIZED,
WE INSCRIBE THIS TRANSLATION
OF A RECORD OF THREE CENTURIES,
WHICH, ADORNED WITH THE
RELIGIOUS GLORIES OF THE OLD WORLD,
INVITES THE NEW
TO PIOUS EMULATION
IN THE CAUSE OF OUR COMMON PATRONESS.

Preface to the Translation

THE present Tercentenary Jubilee which the sodalities of the Blessed Virgin Mary enjoy by a special privilege of His Holiness, Pope Leo XIII., induced Father Louis Delplace, S. J., to compile the historical sketch of which we offer this English translation.[1] The little volume that has thus sprung into existence is at once a dutiful tribute to Her under whose auspices and protection the splendid achievements recorded in its pages were made possible, and a statement of facts that, together with a mass of incidental information, are of interest to all who would rightly estimate the strength and influence of the sodalities in the past three centuries. Besides, it contains an indirect exhortation to the faithful of our day, that they increase the fervor and continue the extension of the venerable institution which has so long verified the scriptural maxim: "Good things continue with their seed, their posterity are a holy inheritance." The trophies of

---

[1] Histoire des Congrégations de la Sainte Vièrge, par le Père L. Delplace, S. J. Souvenir du Jubilé, 1584-1884. Imprimerie du Saint-Augustin : Desclée, de Brouwer et Cie., Lille et Bruges.

the ancestors should arouse their descendants to still greater successes. May there not be some present necessity for heeding this exhortation, if not in the point of numbers, perhaps, in the breadth of the work? May not the spirit of some sodalities be contemplative rather than active — ascetical to the detriment of its apostolic character?

It is to be regretted that the space which Father Delplace allots to sodalities outside of Europe is rather contracted. Those of the United States alone might absorb an important chapter, and present large and edifying statistics. The devout client of the Immaculate who, before the end of the Jubilee year, would gather the materials for a sketch of the sodalities of the Union, to serve as an appendix to this history, would himself most worthily honor his Patroness and foster devotion to her in others.

The translation is the product of a combined effort made by a group of ladies, who are members of a sodality of *Enfants de Marie*. If their ready and successful zeal be an index of the spirit that prevails throughout the sodalities, the speedy diffusion of this memorial volume with its consequent good is assured.

Contents

INTRODUCTION

THE SODALITIES OF THE BLESSED VIRGIN . . . 9

BOOK I

THE FIRST SODALITIES (1563-1584) 11

CHAP.
- I. SODALITIES AT ROME BEFORE 1584 14
- II. THE FIRST SODALITIES OUTSIDE OF ROME . 26
  1. The Sodality at Paris 32
  2. The Sodality at Douay 38
  3. The Sodalities at Cologne and in Germany . . 42
  4. The Sodalities in Bavaria 50
  5. The Sodality of Fribourg 54
  6. The Sodalities at Liège and in the Netherlands, 57

APPENDIX — Bull of Gregory XIII., Granting Special Indulgences to the Sodality of Milan, at the Request of St. Charles Borromeo 64

BOOK II

THE SODALITIES FROM 1584 TO THE SUPPRESSION OF THE SOCIETY OF JESUS IN 1773 68

CHAP.
- I. CANONICAL INSTITUTION OF THE SODALITIES 68

CHAP.		PAGE
II.	DEVELOPMENT AND ORGANIZATION OF THE SODALITIES	76
III.	EXTENSION OF THE SODALITIES, ESPECIALLY IN THE BELGIAN PROVINCES	85
IV.	THE SODALITIES IN THE COLLEGES	95
V.	THE SODALITIES OUTSIDE THE COLLEGES	107
VI.	SODALITIES OF PRIESTS	119
VII.	EXAMPLES OF HOLINESS IN THE SODALITIES,	128
VIII.	PERSECUTIONS AND ENCOURAGEMENTS	143

BOOK III

THE SODALITIES IN THE NINETEENTH CENTURY, 157

CHAP.		
I.	THE SODALITIES FROM THE SUPPRESSION OF THE SOCIETY OF JESUS UNTIL ITS RESTORATION IN 1814	157
II.	THE EXTENSION OF THE SODALITIES SINCE 1814	170
III.	SODALITIES OF STUDENTS	187
IV.	SODALITIES OF MEN	207
V.	IMPORTANCE OF SODALITIES IN OUR DAY	225

APPENDIX — Brief of His Holiness Leo XIII., Granting to all the Sodalities of the Blessed Virgin the Favor of a Jubilee, on the Occasion of the Three Hundredth Anniversary of their Canonical Institution by Gregory XIII. 236

INTRODUCTION

The Sodalities of the Blessed Virgin

1563-1884

ON the fifth of December, 1884, three hundred years will have elapsed since the day when the Apostolic See confirmed and instituted canonically the work of the Sodality of the Blessed Virgin. Though the Sodality of the Roman College, established by Gregory XIII. in advance of all the rest, cannot celebrate its three hundredth anniversary in gladness, but must mingle tears of grief with the sweet memories of its origin, as it did a century ago; yet the children of Mary must not pass over with indifference the memorable date of this third centennial jubilee. Several sodalities in Alsace and Bavaria have lately celebrated the three hundredth anniversary of their foundation; and the festival at Fribourg in 1881 was marked by a magnificence and devotion that won general admiration. The memory of their canonical affiliation to the Sodality of the Roman College cannot fail to arouse in them a renewal of fervor.

We hope that the sodalities now so numerous in the Catholic world will be interested in the historical sketch offered to them in these modest pages. It will give them details concerning the work of the clients of Mary, unimportant, no doubt, in the eyes of the world, but calculated to arouse a feeling of joy and rightful pride in the hearts of faithful sons of the Church, and especially of devout sodalists. They will trace the spirit of the sodalities and gather up blessed memories of an illustrious past, they will feel fresh courage to show themselves worthy of those who have gone before them, and perhaps some zealous servants of Mary may arise, eager to realize the aim of their spiritual union, and add good works and devotion, for the glory of God and the honor of her whom they have chosen for their special Patroness.

Book I

The First Sodalities of the Blessed Virgin

1563-1584

THE Middle Ages produced a great number of associations, which under the name of confraternity, third order, or guild, gathered around the convent or parish church, the faithful of every rank and condition.

"Whoever," says an English author,[1] "can separate himself from the nineteenth century, and read the history of the fourteenth by the light of that period, will allow that confraternities were a powerful element of organization for all that was just and upright: law, morals, civilization, and, we may add, all the higher virtues, found in them valuable support."

The Society of Jesus, raised up by Providence to combat the false Reformation of the sixteenth century, understood from the beginning the power of organization to promote works of piety and

---

[1] Richard Howlett, 1882, "Monumenta Franciscana," Roll Series, vol. II., Preface, p. xxvii.

Christian charity. In the year 1554, Saint Ignatius encouraged Father Salmeron to establish, in the city of Naples, a sodality, whose members proposed to restore, by their example, the habit of frequent communion.[1] At Messina, Father Peter Domenech instituted, during the holy founder's life, the sodality of the Holy Name of Jesus,[2] for the extirpation of blasphemy, and it extended into every country of the globe. Various other associations were founded under Jesuit influence, at Valencia, Messina, and Rome.[3] The principal aim of all was to restore to vigor the habit of frequenting the sacraments, and to organize aid for the poor and sick. But none of these institutions assumed the proportions attained by the sodalities of the Blessed Virgin.

Let us study their beginnings and the spirit that nerved them in the earliest period of their existence. The history of the Company, by Orlandini and his successors, the Annual Letters of the Society of Jesus, printed at Rome ever since the year 1581, and other works or documents from

---

[1] "Historia Societatis Jesu," 1554, 36. This work, begun by Orlandini, and continued by Sacchini and others, is divided into parts, and subdivided into books. Each book corresponds to the history of a complete year; it is enough to indicate the year and number.

[2] H. S., 1554, 72.

[3] H. S., 1554, 71; 1555, 17; 1558, 86.

which we shall give faithful quotations, are the sources of our information. The reader will let us give in detail the early portion of the history of the sodalities; for, the origin of an institution is always interesting. The fruits produced by the sodalities in the first twenty years of their existence, and the remarkable sanctity of the men who helped to found them, seem to us to deserve especial attention.

CHAPTER I

The Sodalities of the Blessed Virgin at Rome before the year 1584

THE sodalities took form and organization in the colleges of the Company of Jesus, and from thence they spread throughout the world, diffusing a salutary influence among all classes of society.

The foundation is usually attributed to the piety of a young Belgian Jesuit, a professor in the Roman College. It is true that in 1562, a devout sodality existed at Perugia among the pupils of the college of the Society.[1] But it does not appear to have been instituted especially in honor of the Mother of God, nor do we find in it any characteristic organization. Father John Bourghois[2] attests in 1620, that the students had formed pious societies in honor of Mary; but they enjoyed no peculiar privileges, and their members belonged to the confraternities of the Holy

---

[1] H. S. 1562, 17.
[2] Soc. Jesu Mariæ ... sacra ... auct. J. Bourghesio, S. J., C. 14. De Bono Sodalitatis Parthenæ, of the same author, chap. I.

Rosary. The Sicilian Jesuits claim for Father Sebastian Cabarasius the honor of having inaugurated the sodalities of the Blessed Virgin.[1] However that may be, the sodality at Rome served as a model for all the rest, and drew up definite rules which were approved later by the Holy See.

John Leonius[2] came from Liége; he was received into the Society by St. Ignatius in 1550, and our holy founder, so say the annals of the Order, formed a favorable judgment of him, which a long career served only to confirm. After completing his first studies in literature and philosophy, he became a teacher of grammar at the Roman College. His zeal inspired him with a desire to develop in his young pupils a love of prayer and spiritual reading; and with this aim he used to join with them in a few devout exercises at the close of the evening classes. These young people became models for the whole college; and other pupils from the lower classes, commonly called grammar and the humanities,[3] joined the pupils

---

[1] Annales Provinciæ Siciliæ S. J., up to the year 1605.

[2] Fisen, S. J., Flores Ecclesiæ Leodiensis: Litteræ Annuæ S. J. 1584, Taurin. Colleg. No document gives the true name of Leonius. We find the Latinized name Leonius; F. Damiens writes Leonis, and the translator gives us Léon and Leonis. Tableau raccourci. Tournai, 1642, p. 184 and p. 428.

[3] Rhetoric was considered as belonging to the higher studies.

of Father Leonius.[1] In the year 1563 they formed the habit of meeting every evening in one of the recitation rooms, where a simple altar had been erected, to recite a few prayers and listen to a short selection from some spiritual book. On Sundays and festivals they chanted vespers in addition to their usual exercises. This incipient work soon assumed the character of a real sodality.

It was in 1564[2] that these young students to the number of seventy, carefully chosen from the Roman College, placed themselves under the special protection of the Blessed Virgin, and drew up their first set of rules. They were substantially as follows: The sodalists proposed, as their aim, progress in piety and in literary pursuits. Every week they went to confession, to purify their hearts from the least stain and to become more pleasing to their Immaculate Patroness; every month, at least, they received the holy eucharist; every day they went to mass and said either the rosary, or certain prayers from the manual of the sodality; at the close of the day's studies, before leaving the college, they made a quarter of an hour's meditation, and for fifteen minutes more pondered over their good resolutions. On Sunday, after chanting vespers and

---

[1] H. S. 1563, 7.   [2] Ibid. 1564, 37.

listening to a short instruction from the father director, they went to the hospitals to console the sick, or performed some other work of charity. A prefect and twelve other officers shared the duty of assisting their young companions with advice, and a father of the Society presided at all the exercises.

Such, according to Sacchini, were the rules that directed the sodality in the beginning, and he adds that, with few variations, they are still observed. The great advantage of these meetings, remarks the same author, was that, by a mutual union in zeal and piety, the members avoided dangerous companionship, and escaped one of the most perilous temptations of youth. Experience soon proved it to be a work inspired by grace for the advancement of study, as well as for progress in virtue. The children of Mary became distinguished everywhere in both connections among their fellow-students. Nothing assists study so much as piety, and, on the other hand, youth, exposed to the fascination of pleasure, and to all sorts of temptations, finds a powerful support in literary studies which captivate mind and imagination with innocent enjoyments, and leave little leisure for idleness and evil suggestions. Moreover, the Mother of Divine Grace, of course, protected her privileged children with tender solicitude, and obtained for them the choicest favors.

The beginnings of the Sodality were modest, but, considering its development and first fruits, we have the testimony of souls devoted to Mary and capable of understanding the graces and blessings that the Holy Virgin poured down upon the young Jesuit's enterprise. The angelic Stanislaus Kostka, who expressed the secret of his love for Mary in those tender words, " She is my mother ; " the venerable Jacob Rem, whom we shall find distinguishing himself by zeal for the sodalities; Claudius Aquaviva, known later as the great promoter of the work, and many other servants of Mary, added distinction to the noviciate of the Company of Jesus about that time, 1566–1567. No doubt, in their spiritual conversations, they interchanged consoling tidings of the work done at the Roman College, and the hopes founded on the growing enterprise.

Meanwhile, Father Leonius was sent to Paris, where we find him in 1569,[1] devoted to the spiritual interests of the Roman troops sent by Pius V. to Charles IX., during the religious wars. But the influence exercised by the sodalities was so salutary that no one dreamed of letting the pious teacher's work languish. It

---

[1] Fisen., op. cit.

was, indeed, now fully developed, and a second sodality was thought necessary in the Roman College, reserved for pupils over eighteen years of age;[1] the same who, six years earlier, had given to the sodality its first humble initiation.

The work being founded for the promotion of belles-lettres as well as of devotion, it soon produced a very important result. In 1569, the students of the Roman College in rhetoric, philosophy, and theology formed the first *Academia* mentioned in the history of the colleges of the Company.[2] It was placed under the benevolent patronage of the Cardinal of Augsburg, one of most devoted protectors of the Order founded by St. Ignatius. These college academies, which have given an effective stimulus to literary studies among the pupils, therefore owe their origin to the sodality of Our Lady. The traditions of the Society record this fact, and the Ratio Studiorum, printed at Rome in 1585, decided, as a general rule of the *Academia*, that only pupils already received into the sodality of the Blessed Virgin should be admitted to these additional literary exercises.[3]

In the following year the academy of the sodality proposed to give, in proof of their literary progress, a representation of a religious drama, " The Prodi-

---

[1] H. S. 1569, 18.   [2] H. S. 1569, 49.   [3] Reg. Acad., 2.

gal Son." But, not having sufficient space for the exhibition, they asked to be allowed to use the great hall of the German College,[1] and were prevented from executing their design by the not very generous rivalry of its students.

Soon after this event both the sodality and the academy were adopted by the Germans themselves, and a more noble emulation was the result. Three sodalities were established among the 135 students of this seminary in 1574; and in this same year, we find a memorial of a literary celebration in both colleges. The German College gave a celebrated tragedy by F. Stephen Tuccio; "Christus Judex," and the numerous spectators received so vivid an impression of the Last Judgment, that their piety was even more satisfied than their curiosity. The sodalist academicians of the Roman College solemnly celebrated the reception of Cardinals Alciati and Paleotti. The former had accepted the office of honorary president after the Cardinal of Augsburg; the latter had established a sodality and academy in the Jesuit College, at Bologna, according to the rules of the Roman College, and he was naturally interested in the young academicians at Rome whom he wished to honor with a visit. Superb decorations, emblems, speeches and poems, all, in

---

[1] H. S. 1570, 9.

short that could express devotion to Mary, and gratitude towards a benefactor, were contributed to celebrate the visit of these august prelates.

These literary exhibitions were afterwards given in regular succession; the members of the four sodalities that flourished at the Roman College in 1581, dividing among themselves the four principal feasts of the Blessed Virgin to honor their patroness with poems and works of oratory. On the Feast of the Annunciation,[1] the foreign Jesuits sent to Rome from various provinces to elect a new general, attended one of these public sessions, and gave their approbation to an institution uniting so wisely devotion to Mary with love of literature. We can have no doubt that the excellent results they saw on this occasion, led to the foundation of sodalities in their respective provinces.

Active and devoted piety, with progress in study, are the principal aim and object of the Sodality, as the history of these early years attests. If, on solemn occasions, literature was sometimes most conspicuous, more often still was Christian charity practised. The sodalists of the Roman College united in the purchase of a great number of articles, during the Holy Week of 1574,[2] for distribution among the poor in Rome and in the

---

[1] Litt. Ann. 1581, Sem. Rom.   [2] H. S. 1574, 9.

Campagna, and for the promotion of devotion to their good Mother. Many of them belonged to noble families; they penetrated to the most squalid quarters to instruct the ignorant in their religious duties, and to bring them to make their Easter confession either at the college church or at the professed house.

About this time, and perhaps after the departure of Leonius, Claudius Aquaviva, while pursuing his course of philosophy and theology, directed the Roman sodalities with characteristic zeal.[1] Three young men of illustrious birth, who were elevated in after-life to the dignity of cardinal, aided in developing and strengthening the work; these were Marianus Perbenedetti, Augustine Valerio, and Octavius Bandini. Ciacconio[2] attributes to them the honor of having founded the Annunziata of the Roman College during their course of philosophy.

Three Generals of the Society encouraged the sodalities. St. Francis Borgia,[3] in particular, animated their fervor by having engraved, in 1569,

---

[1] H. S. 1575, 37. Aquaviva entered the Company of Jesus in 1567, aged 24 years; remained at the Roman College until 1575; after governing the provinces of Naples and Rome, was chosen General in 1581.

[2] Historiæ Pontificum Romanorum et Cardinalium. . . . Romæ, 1677, 4th vol., p. 195.

[3] H. S. 1569, 296.

the first copies of the portrait of the Blessed
Virgin attributed to St. Luke.[1] This engraving
was distributed everywhere, and, two years later,
excited the devotion of the servants of Mary in
the college of Lima in South America,[2] and
led to the establishment of a sodality in that
city. The sodalists owe to the piety of the same
saint, a custom that he had practised in his own
home, and afterwards introduced, for the good of
souls, at the court of King John III. of Portugal.[3]
At the beginning of each month, during one of
the ordinary meetings, each member took at the
foot of the crucifix, a card recommending a particular virtue to practise in imitation of some saint
whom he was to take as his special patron. This
devout habit, as F. Bourghois and F. Crasset[4]
tell us, became common in all the sodalities of
the Blessed Virgin, and aided wonderfully in the
cultivation of Christian virtues.

We do not know in detail the spiritual favors
granted by the Holy See to the Roman sodalities.

---

[1] Vide "La Vierge de Saint Luc," Abbé Anselme Milochan. Paris, Perisse, 1862. "Das Gnadenbild der Mater ter admirabilis von Ingolstadt," Franz Hattler, S. J., Fribourg, Herder, 1880; and the recent work of Father Garrucci " Storia dell' Arte Christiana," vol. III., 13.

[2] H. S. 1571, 227.   [3] Ibid. 1558, 49.

[4] Bourghois, op. cit. chap. XXIII., p. 326; Crasset, Des Cong. de Notre Dame, chap. II.

The sovereign pontiff, Gregory XIII., who succeeded to the pontifical throne in 1572, records in his bull, "Omnipotentis Dei," that he wished to encourage the members of the sodality by giving them special indulgences. But these were only the first marks of approbation, and far more substantial advantages gave to the work of Father Leonius, later, an importance that the humble religious had never dared to anticipate. He thought simply of helping the scholars confided to his care by obedience, to lead a devout life; but in imitation of his foundation in the Roman College, we find everywhere groups of devoted sons of Mary organized into sodalities on a uniform plan, and authoritatively recognized by the sovereign pontiff. If he never enjoyed in this world the sight of this definite organization, at least he had the satisfaction of knowing, through the first annual letters of the Company, printed in 1583, that the sodalities of the Blessed Virgin already existed in many colleges. In the very year when the bull of the foundation of the sodalities appeared, this devoted servant of Mary died at Turin,[1] and received the reward of his zeal in propagating devotion to Our Lady. He was a humble laborer in the Lord's vineyard, and devoted to the poor and sick. He was remembered in the hospital at Turin, taking

[1] Litt. Ann. 1584, Coll. Taurin.

care of an incurable sufferer, whose wounds were so offensive that no one else dared to go near him. Leonius interested himself in this poor creature, and won a victory so complete over nature that he overcame all repugnance and could hardly be persuaded to leave this work of mercy. It is the only trait of his charity handed down by the annals of the company for the consolation and edification of the children of Mary, who were to be distinguished, like their founder, by works of mercy and charity.

While the sodalities of Our Lady were developing at Rome under Leonius and Aquaviva, they were spreading throughout various countries of Europe. We will follow their fortunes in France, Germany, and the Netherlands.

CHAPTER II

The First Sodalities Outside of Rome

FOR half a century heresy had been spreading far and wide, and already menaced France, Germany, and the Low Countries with religious revolt. The Church, in trying to avert the scourge, turned her attention, principally, to the education of the young; considering the organization of seminaries, according to decrees of the Council of Trent, with the foundation of numerous colleges, and a general reform of methods of teaching in the universities, to be the most efficacious means to prevent propagation of the evil. Through the education of youth, the great work of Catholic Reform was to be inaugurated and completed, and the sodalities were destined to take an important share in this.

One of the earliest and most zealous promoters of this institution in our countric., Father Costerus, will tell us the aim proposed in establishing sodalities of the Blessed Virgin.

Francis Costerus was born at Malines, in 1531,

and was received into the Society of Jesus, at twenty-one years of age, by St. Ignatius himself.[1] While still very young, he was sent from Rome to Cologne,[2] to teach in the college of the Three Crowns, which the authorities of the city wished to confide to the care of the Company. He was a distinguished professor of Holy Scripture, a master of novices,[3] and a formidable preacher against heresy, displaying in that famous city such energetic zeal as to earn the surname of the Scourge of Lutheranism.[4] After governing the province of Belgium for six years,[5] he was successively made rector of the colleges of Bruges[6] and Cologne,[7] superior of the Rhenish[8] province, and, later, of the Belgian.[9] He was especially distinguished in the annals of his order by his devout and touching trust in Mary, shown in his numerous writings, and proved again and again in the course of his long and holy career. In 1617,[10] when he was giving last words of counsel to a noble youth, Charles de Grobbendonck, whom he was taking to the noviciate of Malines, Costerus, then eighty-six years old, gave him the same

---

[1] Societas Jesu Mariæ Sacra, chap. 19.   [2] H. S., 1556, 26.
[3] Ibid., 1557, 26.   [4] Ibid., 1565, 51.
[5] Ibid., 1573, 97.   [6] Ibid., 1574, 60.
[7] Ibid., 1575, 127.   [8] Ibid., 1580, 179.
[9] Ibid., 1585, 128.
[10] Nadasi, "Annales Mariani," n. 1112, p. 516.

advice that he himself had received, so long ago, from St. Ignatius: "My son," he said, "be always humble and obedient, and you will find joy and happiness. May the Blessed Virgin obtain this triple blessing for you, and preserve your health as she has mine." The good old man added: "When I was leaving Rome, and St. Ignatius recommended to me joy of the soul, I asked myself, in some anxiety, how I could preserve it if sickness should force me to be unemployed? But the Blessed Virgin gave me to understand that if I would be faithful to obedience and humility she would take care of my health. Now remember that she has kept her promise, and that if you ever hear that Father Costerus is an invalid, do not believe a word of it; it will be a lie, and an insult to our good Mother. My first sickness and my death will come very near together." The prediction was verified in 1619, after a career of more than seventy years consecrated to the service of Holy Church.

According to the testimony of F. Bourghois, Costerus tried to found everywhere sodalities of the Blessed Virgin. Not only was he a most ardent propagandist, but he devoted his pen to the service of this work; the various writings that he left behind him in praise of the sodalities give us details of their history that we find nowhere else.

It was in 1576, according to Sotwell, that he edited, under the title "Bulla Professionis Fidei," a little work, which was reprinted many times, and usually, since 1586, under a new title, "Libellus Sodalitatis Beatæ Mariæ Virginis,"[1] a manual of the sodality. Three other works of piety or controversy, published by the same author for the use of the sodalists at Cologne, Douay, and Antwerp, enable us to appreciate the spirit of these institutions in the provinces of the North.

"To prevent the encroachment of error among the rising generation and secure to them a Christian education," writes Costerus in the preface to the "Libellus Sodalitatis," "in this lies the salvation of Catholic countries. Now," he adds, "it is not difficult to keep young people in the path of duty while they are obedient to their teachers; but their souls must be so penetrated with piety and fired with divine love, that they will voluntarily devote themselves to study and to morality, and in after-life use for the good of their neighbor the virtues acquired during their college course. Therefore the Company believed," he continues, "that in addition to frequenting the

---

[1] De Backer in his "Bibliographie des Écrivains de la Compagnie de Jésus," cites eleven Latin editions, one German translation, and three Flemish; seven French editions under the titles, "Livre de la Compagnie, . . . de la Confrérie, . . . de la Congrégation."

sacraments and daily attendance at mass, it would be well for the pupils to be united by common rules in a voluntary association, where they would learn to guide themselves, and be drawn to a devout Christian life by bonds voluntarily assumed, learning by force of example and mutual encouragement to make public profession of piety and Christianity. It seemed well to place this association under the protection and patronage of the Blessed Virgin. . . . The partisans of the Reformation invariably attack the Holy Virgin, who has overcome all heresies. It is not without reason that the serpent tries to wound the foot that crushed his head, and that the dragon pursues the woman who has driven the prince of this world from his domain. . . . She was therefore chosen patroness of the sodality that she might take care of the young people and show herself their sovereign and mother, by granting them success in developing their talents, a will disposed to virtue, and courage to help their neighbor." Then, having enumerated the countries especially consecrated to the Blessed Virgin, citing in particular the dioceses of Cambray, Tournay, Arras, and Tongres, he continues, "The most holy mother of Jesus Christ, who has taken so many nations under her protection, should be the patroness of youth, for the very reason that the heretics try to crush the glory of Mary. Luther and the Centuriators of Magdeburg place her below the most infamous beings. Adopting the opinion of an impious emperor, Constantine Copronymus, they admit that though she was great, inasmuch as she bore in her womb the Son of God, yet she afterwards became subject to vice and sin like the most vulgar sinners. Christians — and, above all, young students — must not tolerate such blasphemies. They must avenge these outrages; they must honor and venerate the Mother of God and Queen of mankind."

These few extracts from the preface of the Libellus show clearly that under the direction of F. Costerus the sodalities were principally directed against the heresy which afflicted the church in our countries. The prefaces of the smaller works dedicated by the same author to the sodalists of Douay and Antwerp breathe the same ideas as the "Libellus Sodalitatis." In confirmation of our impression we will add two remarks. First, we read at the beginning of these various works of F. Costerus, the profession of faith formulated by the Council of Trent against Protestant errors,[1]

[1] A public profession of faith, in accordance with the proposal of Blessed Canisius, had been made obligatory throughout Italy for all teachers. (H. S. 1564, 40.) This custom, introduced in the University of Ingolstadt (Ib. 1568, 130) in spite of eager opposition, was adopted in most universities, greatly to the advantage of Catholic education.

and all sodalists, from the time of their admission, were obliged to give public adherence to this creed. Secondly, the act of consecration uttered even in our own day, by those who are admitted to the sodalities, and which we find in identical terms at the beginning of the "Libellus Sodalitatis," seems to have been drawn up as a protest against the insults directed by heretics against the Mother of God; the servants of Mary promising "never to allow their inferiors to say or do anything contrary to her honor.

To avert the scourge of heresy, revive the Catholic faith by devotion to Mary, lead back nations to the frequent reception of the sacraments, and preserve the young especially from the seduction of error and make them apostles by word and example, — such were the aims and advantages offered by the sodalities in countries menaced by Protestantism.

1. The Sodality at Paris.

Sacchini tells us that the first sodality was that of Douay;[1] but F. Costerus states positively that the sodality of the college of Clermont at Paris[2] was already in a flourishing condition and bearing

---

[1] H. S. 1573, 96. Nadasi. op. cit. n. 240, says it was the first one affiliated to that of Rome.

[2] Liber Sodalitatis, preface.

good fruit when he himself established the one at Douay. It even appears to have owed its existence to F. Leonius, judging by the words of F. Fisen in his " Fleurs de l'Église de Liège ; " for he says " In the capital of France he propagated devotion to Mary with the same ardor and with equal success, beginning always with young people." From the beginning, this sodality had a good share of the difficulties that the University always brought upon the Society: as we shall see in a letter addressed in 1575 to the Sovereign Pontiff, Gregory XIII., by F. Claude Mathieu, Provincial of France.[1] After mentioning the calumnies and persecutions directed against the teaching of the Jesuits by certain doctors of the Sorbonne, imbued with Calvinistic opinions, F. Claude Mathieu continues thus: " Why should they dissuade men from frequenting the sacraments? Why does Dr. Pelletier, in public and private discourse, inveigh against the sodality of the Blessed Virgin, approved by the Holy See, and productive of great benefit to the pupils of our schools? Why will they not admit to the Sorbonne those who are members of this devout sodality?" These complaints plainly show that heresy looked with an evil eye on an institution

---

[1] Maldonat et l'Université de Paris, par le P. Prat S. J. pièces justificatives, p. 597.

consecrated to devotion to Our Lady, and to the practice of a Christian life. But if it could not please the partisans of error, it realized none the less great good. Thanks to the good example of the sodalists, piety increased among the pupils of the college at Clermont, and Catholic families sent thither more children than it could receive.

It was about the time of this period of persecution that the young Francis de Sales, destined by his father to the college of Navarre, by entreaties won permission to go to that of Clermont, to learn, as he said, the sciences and the road to Heaven both together, and avoid the dangers from which his virtue recoiled. He was only thirteen years old when, in 1580, he began the course of rhetoric. His piety gained for him admission to the sodality, where for six years he was distinguished for his zeal and good example. He was judged worthy of the first rank in it, was chosen for the posts of assistant and of prefect, the highest in the sodality, and was re-elected again and again when his time of government service expired. Indeed Francis looked upon these charges as an apostolate, and labored with all his soul for the good of the members of this fervent society, speaking to them in public and private, and helping them with good advice. He took no less pains with youths who wished to enter the sodality, and led them to look on their admission as a special favor, for which they were to prepare by the means he pointed out. Thus the association was always recruited with exemplary subjects, and became from day to day more fervent. Everyone has read in the history of his life how the Blessed Virgin delivered him from a frightful temptation to despair that took possession of him while he was at Clermont,[1] when finding at the foot of the statue of Mary the "Remember, O most Holy Virgin Mary!" he drew from that consoling prayer an unlimited confidence in the Mother of our Saviour. The holy prefect of the sodality must have exercised great influence over its members. The King of France, Henry III., one day visited these young students formed in part by his generous zeal, and listening to the prayer to the Blessed Virgin with which the school closed, said to the rector with a sense of consolation for the evils of heresy, "Thank God, at least these will never be heretics."[2]

While the sodality of Clermont was training an illustrious servant of the Blessed Virgin and a great doctor of the church, a new one was forming which no doubt was even more dreaded by the reformers, on account of the influence of

---

[1] Vie de Saint François de Sales by Hamon, vol. I. chap. III.
[2] Litt. Ann. 1582; Domus et Coll. Paris.

its members. The penitents of the Annunciation of Our Lady, with the King for patron and the Cardinal de Bourbon for president, were instituted by F. Edmond Augier.[1] The profession of faith made by them on entering, their general statutes and those of "the second and strict rule," above all, the motives of the institution, give us an idea of the aim of that sodality. We give a few lines from it :[2] "It has pleased the king to honor this sodality of Our Lady for three reasons: first, that his majesty has always had a great devotion to the Queen of Heaven; ... the other that our God has been so generous towards this poor world, destitute of all means of saving itself, that he has generously given his own son ... we could not find a patron or model of all piety and liberality to the poor more attractive or of so heavenly generosity; thirdly, it has been our common hope to see some day, in this kingdom, the death and overthrow of all the heresies, errors, and false opinions that distract it, through the ardent prayers of the Blessed Virgin, so that the church may sing, 'Gaude, Maria Virgo, cunctas hæreses sola interemisti in universo mundo.' Every member shall hear mass every day, unless

---

[1] His life was written by Bailly; De Backer Bibliographie.

[2] Cimber, Archives curieuses de l'Histoire de France. 1st series, t. X. p. 442.

there be just cause to the contrary; each shall promise that God shall not be offended in his family . . . he shall say daily the chaplet of Our Lady, or at least one decade; . . . he shall visit prisoners and get them to hear mass, preach to them, or engage for them a preacher; console them, and if there be among them any who are condemned to death, not leave them until they are led from the prison to execution. The same applies to hospitals."

The college of Clermont, so celebrated later under the name of Louis le Grand, produced more than ordinary good Christians. A contemporary wrote:[1] "As to the strictest religious houses, such as those of the Carthusians, Capuchins, and Minims, it may be said with truth that the college at Paris is their common seminary. . . To this end, moreover, the sodality of Our Lady established in the said college, has greatly served. Here we find, in addition to a great number of young pupils, many doctors, prelates, councillors, advocates, and merchants. The exhortations are usually given by great theologians; meditations penances, confessions, and communions are very frequent. The spirit of devotion is easily maintained by means of high masses and vespers, with

[1] Carayon, Documents inédits concernant la Compagnie de Jésus, t. I

music and great solemnities on Sundays and holy days; King Charles IX., King Henry III., the queens, princesses, bishops, and peers of the court of parliament, not disdaining to attend the little chapel of this great college."

2. The Sodality at Douay.

In 1569 F. Costerus, as provincial of Belgium, accepted the college of the Company of Jesus at Douay,[1] a foundation made by the Benedictines of Anchin. As he had nothing more at heart than confirming devotion to the Blessed Virgin, he founded there, in 1573, the first sodality in the Belgian province. It was approved by the Bishop of Arras, François Richardot, and about the year 1581 entered into a communication of privileges with the Sodality of the Annunciation, founded at the Roman College.[2]

The change wrought at once by this fervent society in the conduct of the pupils, their piety, their enthusiasm for study, the influence of its members on their companions, became evident to all. From that time most of the students, we are told, in a little work dedicated to them by the devout Jesuit, in 1587, approached the sacraments of penance

---

[1] Buzelin, "Societas Jesu Gallo-Belgica," 423.
[2] "De Vita et Laudibus Deiparæ," by Costerus, preface, p. 22; a work reprinted in the Summa aurea of the Coll. Migne.

and the eucharist every week, and labored earnestly for the salvation of souls.

"By the grace of God and favor of the Virgin Mary," he adds, "many young men, who are members of this sodality, have already rendered important services to the Christian religion, some in civil professions and others in the ecclesiastical state; many have entered religion; its fame and the fruits of salvation that it has produced are spread throughout Germany." Indeed, the College of Douay received youths from all the northern countries, so extensive was its reputation in a few years.

Meantime persecution was let loose against the College of Anchin, and, after furnishing a refuge to the Jesuits expelled from Cambrai and Tournai, it was for a short time dispersed, in 1578, by a band of Protestant sectarians, in spite of the magistrates' efforts. Three weeks later, when it was reopened by the intervention of the university and civil authorities, six sons of the sodality fell victims to their devotion in a time of pestilence. But the founder of the sodality of Douay might be consoled in these trials and losses when he learned, in 1582,[1] that out of the twenty-eight classes in theology, philosophy, and the humanities, thirty sodalists, either priests or masters

---

[1] Litt. Ann., 1532, Coll. Duac., p. 219.

of art, entered the Company at one time; and when, four years later, he was provincial of Belgium,[1] and received the offer of thirty-three pupils of Douay to become sons of St. Ignatius, of whom he admitted only twenty-four. This was the reward of his zeal for the work of the sodalities; for them it was the most precious favor that Mary can obtain from God for her children of predilection. In those unhappy times, when heresy menaced faith, Mary watched over that country, and multiplied religious and sacerdotal vocations among her devoted servants. The clergy had been too few to resist error effectually.

Among the six hundred students who went to the college of Douay at that time,[2] three sodalities were formed: two for pupils, and a third for the religious of the Abbey of Anchin. In the preface of the book that he dedicated to them,[3] Costerus encouraged them to show their love to the Blessed Virgin, to maintain and diffuse devotion to her, in opposition to heretics, the contemners of the Mother of Christ: "and because," said he, "among the prayers that the sodalists recite in honor of their patroness, the principal devotion is the one which is usually called the Rosary, consisting of five Paters and five Aves,"

[1] H. S. 1586, 60.   [2] Litt. Ann., 1584. Coll. Duac.
[3] De vita et laudibus Deiparæ, pref. p. 14.

he placed at the beginning of his book twenty propositions communicated to him by the sodality of the Blessed Virgin at Mayence, that they might learn to say these prayers with more devotion and defend them against the attacks of their enemies. These propositions consist in a forcible justification of the use of the rosary against heretics. The catechism of Malines, of which the first edition appeared in 1609, gives us in the nineteenth lesson a similar justification, a lasting proof of the absurd calumnies directed by the Protestant heresy against this holy exercise, perhaps, because it was too accessible to the piety of the poor and ignorant faithful.

The work of Costerus is composed of fifty meditations on the virtues of the Virgin Mary. His is not the only testimony that we have of the habit that prevailed among fervent sodalists of consecrating some time each day to the solid and admirable practice of mental prayer. It is for their use that Scribani, Busæus, and Haineufve composed the books of meditation that were so often reprinted[1] and the popularity of which is attested by Boileau when he condemns in one of

[1] In the edition of 1629 (Douay), dedicated to Étienne Werber, "episcopo Mysiensi, qui 28 annos præfuit sodalitati Moguntinæ," the preface says: Post tot meditationes patrum S. J. . . . breviores vel longiores in partheniorum gratiam (quibus congregationis leges non semel hoc pium exercitium commendant.) . . .

his epistles the works of less fortunate authors, to —

> " . . . couvrir chez Thierry d'une feuille encor neuve
> Les méditations de Busée et d'Haineuve."

3. THE SODALITIES AT COLOGNE AND IN GERMANY.

After Douay, Cologne enjoyed the benefit of F. Costerus' zeal. The college of the Three Crowns had in 1575, more than six hundred pupils; it had been cruelly tried by the premature death of its rector, Leonard Kessel, who with F. Jean Rhetius, and a house servant, was assassinated by a poor wretch attacked with insanity.[1] The loss of so devoted a rector seemed irreparable, unless by the return of the father who had inaugurated the school with him. Costerus was therefore recalled from Bruges, where he was organizing courses in the humanities with the generous aid of the Bishop Remi Drieux.[2] In the first year of his stay at Cologne he founded two sodalities at once, that of the Blessed Sacrament and that of the Blessed Virgin.[3] The latter was immediately approved by Gaspard Gropperus, the Papal Nuncio.

[1] H. S. 1574, 58.
[2] Notice historique sur l'ancien collège des Jésuites à Bruges, ch. ii. in the Annales de la Société d'Émulation, t. xxxiv., 1884.
[3] Ib. 1575, 127.

After the diploma of foundation, come the principal rules for its government.[1]

1st. This sodality is instituted in honor of the Blessed Virgin Mary, that the students, by attaching themselves to the most holy Mother of God with especial devotion, may receive from her a special assistance in their studies and conduct.

2d. All must recite, before admission, the profession of faith formulated by the Council of Trent, and be inscribed in the confraternity of the Rosary, in the church of the Friars-preachers. We desire this sodality to be, as it were, a section or member of that confraternity.

3d. All the members will go to confession every week; they will receive holy communion every month, and also on the festivals of the Blessed Virgin, namely, the Purification, the Annunciation, the Visitation, the Assumption, the Nativity, and the Conception of Mary; on the feasts of Easter, the Ascension, Pentecost, the Holy Sacrament, All Saints, and Christmas, unless their confessors find some objection. Every day they will recite the chapter of the Blessed Virgin; and moreover, on Sundays and the above-named festivals, and on the feasts of the Holy Apostles and of the Nativity of St. John the Baptist, they will

---

[1] Reiffenberg S. J. Historia Provinciæ S. J. ad Rhenum, Mantissa diplomatum, p. 53.

recite the office of the Virgin, excepting those who are bound to say the great office. They will recite every morning the Ave Maris Stella, and in the evening the anthem, Salve Regina.

5th. Let them learn to serve mass, and to ask of the prefect of the sodality, or of their confessor, the way to pray, make their confession, and receive Holy Communion.

6th. They will avoid bad company, blasphemy, and evil conversations; they will preserve modesty and courtesy for the edification of others, as becomes devoted servants of the Blessed Virgin; and those who are students will be zealous for the observance of the rules of the college. Anyone who behaves ill, after a third admonition, will be dismissed from the sodality. For this reason, and that the sodality may preserve its purity, no one will be admitted until he has been tested, and has given proofs of perseverance; nor will he be retained if he should fall into a grievous fault.

9th. The meetings will be held every Sunday, and on the Feasts of the Blessed Virgin; matters will be treated that concern the good of the sodality and of the members.

The other rules give prayers to be recited for the sick and for the dead; also the numerous indulgences attached to works of piety, to examination of conscience, communions, etc.

The history of the college of Cologne throws light on some customs peculiar to that sodality.[1] Every month the sodalists elected a prefect for each class, whose duty it was to reprove kindly anyone who had failed in his duties; and in each *hospitium*, as the private houses were called where foreign students lived, they chose a censor, or tutor, to divide the hours of work, and watch over the conduct of his companions. On the first of every month, the members placed themselves under the protection of a saint whose virtues they were to study and imitate.

Costerus took pleasure in seeing the rapid progress that these young students made in literary proficiency as well as in piety, thanks to their mutual encouragement. To reward them and interest them still more, he edited in the following year (1576), the first book that was published for the sodalities of the Blessed Virgin. In it he explained the duties of the sodalists, and pointed out various ways of putting their zeal in practice. At the beginning of the work we find the bull of Pius IV., and the profession of Catholic faith prescribed therein for doctors of theology and converted heretics. "This little work," says the author, in a subsequent edition,[2] "was exhausted

---

[1] Reiffenberg, op. cit., B. VII., ch. 1 and 2.
[2] Libel. Sodal. ed. 1586, preface.

so soon, that it had to be reprinted many times and in various places, and translated into several languages. I was surprised, for I had only written it for our pupils, and in a rather careless style. However, my work has proved attractive and useful, even to older persons, who say that it has been quite beneficial to them."

The work of this zealous director received, in 1577, the more important approbation of the sovereign pontiff. In the diploma confirming the sodality of Cologne, Gregory XIII. granted an indulgence of twenty years to those who should inculcate any point of the instructions contained in the manual, such as the method of confession and examination of conscience, the manner of hearing mass, the meaning of the ceremonies of the Church, etc.[1] This was, of course, very encouraging to the sodalists, whose zeal came to the aid of their teachers in reclaiming heretics and wavering Catholics. Their charitable practices, especially as regarded the faithful who had been seduced into error; the public recitation of the litany of the Blessed Virgin, their pilgrimages, — all, in short, that heresy treated as superstitious practices, — gave the more edification because their public profession of piety was united to an exemplary life.

[1] An ext. from this diploma, dated Sept. 10, 1577, is found at the beginning of the Libellus.

The work developed admirably at Cologne, and exercised so wide an influence that the preservation of the Catholic faith in that famous city of the Rhine has been generally attributed to it. So Costerus himself testifies in his works.[1] It is true, as he tells us, that he received important aid from distinguished members of the clergy and from the Apostolic Nuncio, Barthélemi de Portia. "This prince of the church, who deserves our eternal gratitude," he writes, "inscribed himself and his whole household among the number of the sodalists. By the protection of the Blessed Virgin, their zeal inspired the city council with a generous determination to maintain the Catholic faith in its purity, in spite of the immense obstacles raised by the Lutherans, and in spite of the scandal caused by the apostasy of Archbishop Gebhard Truchses in 1583. This prelate tried in vain to carry his clergy with him into apostasy, and if he had succeeded, the Protestant princes of Germany would have "secured a plurality of votes, as they would have had four out of seven, beside that of the archbishop of Mayence, who seemed inclined towards that party."[2] The supremacy of the Austrian House would then have merged into a Protestant House. A great num-

---

[1] Libellus Sodalitatis, Preface.
[2] Mémoires de Mornay, II., 280.

ber of priests enrolled themselves in the pious association of Cologne. The Abbot of St. Trond joined it in 1582, with twelve of his religious. Another religious community of men, driven from Amsterdam and settled in Wesel, entered that same year.[1] Five sodalities had been established among the numerous students of the Three Crowns College. They were about a thousand, among them a hundred boarders, most of them of Belgian extraction, but obliged, owing to religious troubles, to be educated in a foreign land.[2] The sodality was the soul of that establishment. The influence of those who were admitted by Costerus made itself felt in the very midst of them all, and inaugurated a movement supremely favorable to virtue and to literary progress. Their operations, however, were not confined within the college enclosure. Some distinguished themselves by their ardor in teaching catechism, others exercised their zeal against heresy by destroying the works of Luther and Erasmus.[3] Some of the

---

[1] Litt. Ann., Coll. Colon., 1582, p. 170.

[2] Ibid. 1585, p. 271.

[3] It is interesting to see how this celebrated writer was judged by the pupils and their Catholic masters at Cologne. An ex-Augustinian like Luther, afterwards secretary to Henri de Bergues, bishop of Cambray, a fiery opponent of the Scholastic Philosophy, dependent on the liberality of princes and of the Pope — disregard of whose dignity he denounced as an impiety, — on excellent terms

older ones were true apostles, as active as missionaries; and "one was astonished," so say the Annals of the College, "that so many of these young men, brought up in the midst of the Lutheran errors, should not have been contaminated." It was owing to the spirit of zeal imparted to them by the sodality, that pushed them onward to action and to struggle; not satisfied with merely defending themselves against the dangers of heresy, they learned how to take the offensive against their formidable adversaries. Apostles from their youth, they consecrated themselves in large numbers to an apostolic life, in the secular clergy and religious orders. Cologne, like Douay, became a nursery of zealous priests, who protected their faith — the true one — against the power of Lutheranism.

From Cologne, where they were productive of so much consolation among the pupils, the sodalities of the Blessed Virgin spread in all the Rhenish province.[1] The colleges of Trèves, of Würz-

with Luther and Melanchthon, full of wavering notions about the Church and about the Reformation, the precursor and hierophant of the modern spirit, as M. Durand de Laur styles him, — Erasmus nevertheless died as a Christian, and was assisted in his last moments by a priest of Turnhout. (De Ram, Bulletins de l'Académie Royale de Belgique, IX., 462; Annuaire de l'Université de Louvain, 1852.)

[1] Litt. Ann., 1581, Coll. Trevir., p. 175.

burg, of Mayence, of Fulda, of Speyer, of Coblentz, thanks to the zeal of Father Costerus, welcomed the work and witnessed its progress, before it received its final organization from Rome. The College of Molsheim in Alsace, founded in 1580, at the request of Jean de Manderscheid, the bishop of Strasburg, had, from the beginning, a sodality which distinguished itself by its activity against heretical attacks, and was the cradle of all those formed in Alsace.[1]

4. THE SODALITIES IN BAVARIA.

Bavaria, which the Reformation tried twenty times to invade, was saved from heresy by the Society of Jesus. Paul Hoffæus and the blessed Peter Canisius, distinguished not only for their devotion to the Blessed Virgin, but also for their scientific and oratorical talents, rendered themselves so famous by their zeal, that the Duke Albert compared it to that of the apostles. He applied to them the praise that the church addresses to the first preachers of the gospel: Petrus Apostolus et Paulus, ipsi nos docuerunt legem tuam, Domine.[2]

[1] Four years since, this sodality celebrated the Tercentenary of its institution in a style of magnificence of which a detailed report may be found in the Catholic paper, "L'Union d'Alsace-Lorraine," for Aug. 9, 1880.

[2] H. S., Book XXV., 3.

There has recently been written a history of the Bavarian sodalities, by M. Sattler.[1] The first, that of Dillingen, owed its origin to the venerable Father Jacob Rem.[2] Whilst yet a novice in Rome, in 1566, he had witnessed the zeal of Leonius for the honor of Mary, and the salutary influence that this new work exercised over the minds of the young students. Becoming professor, or prefect, of St. Jerome's College, in Dillingen, he took to heart the spreading of the devotion to the Blessed Virgin, by means of the sodality. He had met one of those young men whose talents and virtues when at college, influenced in favor of what was good. Wolfgang Sigismund Haunsperg, belonging to a noble Bavarian family, took advantage of his social position to assist in Father Rem's scheme. In 1576 he formed a party of twenty-five select boarders, all of them decided, like himself, to give to the young men of the college the example of piety and application, and put it under the patronage of Mary. As the heretics had particularly discredited the devotion of the Holy Rosary, they got their names inscribed

---

[1] Geschichte der Marianischen Congregationen in Bayern. Munich, 1864.

[2] The life of this venerable servant of Mary has been written with equal erudition and piety by F. Fr. Hattler, S. J., Der ehrwürdige P. Jacob Rem und seine Marienconferenz, von Fr. Hattler, S. J., Regensburg, Georg Manz. 1881.

in the confraternity of that name, and engaged themselves never to allow a day to pass without reciting their beads.[1]

In the following year, Father Rem had the consolation of seeing this fervent sodality become so large that it had to be divided into two sections. During the eight years that he lived in Dillingen, the colleges of Ingolstadt, of Munich, of Halle, of Innspruck, and of Lucerne welcomed a work, which so marvellously aided in the education of young men. In 1579, Father Anthony Possevin, who was sent to Stockholm by the Sovereign Pontiff to confirm in the Catholic faith the King of Sweden, was ordered to convey a particular bull to these different sodalities, which Gregory XIII. ratified, and in which he granted them great indulgences.[2]

These many favors encouraged the children of Mary; but not the least favorable to the development of the work, was the earnestness with which Catholics in the highest ranks of society, princes of the church, and even the secular sovereigns, furthered its growth. In Munich, in 1579, whilst, under the direction of Father Caspar Hayvodus, the young Joachim von Fugger presided at one of their regular reunions, in the capacity of pre-

[1] Agricola, Hist. Prov. Germ. Sup., p. 169.
[2] Ibid., p. 197.

fect, William, son of Albert V., and hereditary prince of the duchy of Bavaria, came to solicit the favor of being admitted as a member of the sodality, and like them he solemnly promised love and fidelity to the mother of Jesus Christ. His son, Maximilian, was, four years later, prefect of that sodality. He then secured his brother Philip, who became, later on, Bishop of Ratisbonne, and cardinal; also many other young men of the most illustrious families in Bavaria, who, after having made their profession of faith, constituted themselves the perpetual servants and defenders of the Blessed Virgin.

Who will ever be able fully to appreciate the good these thousands of young men did for the maintenance of the Catholic faith in Bavaria, brought up as they were in religious exercises and with sentiments of piety and devotion to the Blessed Virgin? "It is a glory for Dillingen," says the historian from whom we borrow these details, "to have inaugurated these sodalities, which, later on, could generally count up thirty thousand men[1] and youths as their members, in the single province of Upper Germany."

[1] Agricola, Hist. Prov. Germ. Sup. p. 169.,

5. THE SODALITY OF FRIBOURG.

Fribourg had its sodality of the Blessed Virgin since 1581, and it was the blessed Peter Canisius who founded it. He had barely arrived in that city, where he was to pass the last seventeen years of his long and fruitful life, when the saint judged that, in order to dispel heresy, which threatened Fribourg from all parts, nothing would prove more efficacious than to promote the devotion of the Blessed Virgin. Even before opening an educational establishment, he instituted a sodality of young men, and admitted it into that of the Roman College. The names of the first dignitaries have been preserved in a document which may be found in the archives of the public library of Fribourg. These were Pancrace Python, whose nephew later on wrote the life of Bl. Peter, and two young men belonging to the highest nobility, Nicolas Mayer and Charles de Diesbach.[1] General confession, communion, the day of one's reception, daily examination of one's conscience, meetings every two weeks, visiting sick members,

---

[1] Boero, Vita del B. P. Canisio, p. 379. The details which follow in our text, are drawn from the "General Rules or Constitutions of the Sodality of Our Lady of the Assumption," a German manuscript of 34 pages, which the Sodality of Fribourg preserves with religious care, and which was exhibited in 1882, on the occasion of the tercentenary of its foundation.

devotion to the patrons of the month, were exercises which the association of Fribourg (as elsewhere) furthered and recorded in the very first of its rules. Let us only notice the great importance given to the part assigned to the prefect and consulters of that sodality. They do not merely possess an honorary title,—their actions are well defined, subordinate, however, to the management of the Father Director. The young men who are acknowledged worthy of being admitted, and who have attained the proper age (twenty years), have to be instructed by one of the assistants, for one or two months, in their future obligations. In the council which convenes every month, the two assistants, the secretary, the two consulters, and the prefect deliberate with the director as to the admission of postulants, and on whatever tends to the advancement and good government of the sodality. The prefect gives, with the approbation of the father, the certificate of admission countersigned by the secretary. He puts the seal of the sodality on the register of expenses. The assistants and he "are one heart, one soul—by their vigilance and affability they will remove obstacles from their way." If any one of the members of the sodality is ill, the prefect will see that he is visited and consoled by his colleagues, who, besides, will watch that he receives the last sacraments in seasonable time. The second part of the rule, settles on four great meetings during the year, among others on the 8th of September, "at midday in the church of Notre Dame of Bourguillon, to thank God and his ever blessed Mother for having afforded us the privilege of having the sodality, which, after having originated in Rome, was introduced in Fribourg by the very Rev. John Francis Bonhomius, legate of the Apostolic See, and by the much beloved and very learned nobleman and Father, Dr. Peter Canisius, who established it there on the day of the Nativity of the Blessed Virgin Mary, in the year 1581." On Good Friday, after matins in the evening, the college sodality, and the four other sodalities established for men, young men, and girls, moved in slow and solemn procession from the church of Notre Dame to St. Nicholas, to visit the holy sepulchre, and from there to the Franciscan church. The cross was carried at the head of the *cortège*, then followed the young men, the citizens, the nobility, and the city authorities, after whom came the prefect accompanied by the councillors of the state. The second part of the *cortège* was composed of women, preceded by the prefectess and her assistants. Each one carried a lighted taper. Five Our Fathers and five Hail Marys were recited, with the arms crossed, before the Consecrated Host. On the way, the Lord's passion was meditated upon. The Holy Virgin, who has overcome all heresies in making them powerless against the church, especially protected Fribourg. The witnesses who were summoned in the Beatification of the blessed Peter Canisius, gave evidence that the sodality was the great means by which Providence helped to keep the Catholic faith intact in that city.[1] We know what the heretics of Geneva aimed at. The inhabitants of Fribourg, most distinguished for their piety, have for three centuries considered, and do still consider it, a great honor to be ranked under the banner of the children of Mary.

6. THE SODALITY AT LIÉGE AND IN THE NETHERLANDS.

In the midst of the religious troubles and the calamities of all kinds, which afflicted the Province of Belgium from 1566 until 1585, the colleges of the Society had not found the tranquillity necessary to the work of education. Thanks to the energy of the Prince-bishop, Cardinal Gérard de Groesbeck, the district of Liége enjoyed comparative peace. As early as 1569, the Society of Jesus had sent some of its children to exercise the

[1] Riess Der Selige Petrus Canisius, p. 474.

holy ministry in the capital of that principality; their devotion, especially during the ravages of the plague in 1579, had won for them a very honorable record, and the council had masses celebrated in the thirty-two parishes of the city for their superior, F. Nicholas Menu de Dinant, who had sacrificed his life to the service of the sick, with two other members of the Society.[1] It is probable that a sodality of the Blessed Virgin was founded about that time at Liége; for, in 1579, there appeared an edition of the first treatise that Costerus had edited, at Cologne, three years before, for the use of members of the confraternity. The fruits reaped thence by the Jesuits are enumerated in a letter which the Prince-bishop, Ernest de Bavière, wrote in 1581 to the general of the society, Claudius Aquaviva: "Such has been," said he, "the good done by them, that the principality of Liége alone remained faithful to the Catholic faith, while all the neighboring provinces have fallen into heresy." Therefore, wishing to develop the results already acquired, he confirmed the grants made by his predecessor, and definitely established the college. The sodality formed amongst the pupils, according to the rules of that at Cologne, bore, like all the others, fruits of bene-

[1] H. S. 1579, 131.

diction and of holiness.[1] The one that Father Costerus founded at Bruges in 1575 enjoyed but a passing existence; the Jesuits had to yield to the partisans of the Prince of Orange, who, in the name of religious liberty, suppressed the college. It was only re-established after the submission of the city to its legitimate sovereign, Philip II.

St. Omer saw a sodality started among its six hundred scholars in 1582. The principal citizens, and the bishop with a part of his clergy, wished to become members of it, and the Lettres Annuelles have kept the remembrance of the courageous steps which they took before the authorities to prevent the expulsion of the Jesuits, after the latter had refused to take the oath of allegiance to the Duke d'Alençon.[2] The same letters render homage to the zeal which they displayed to revive the receiving of the sacraments: thanks to their example, there were soon seen, every Sunday, from three to five hundred of the faithful partaking of the Blessed Eucharist in the college church. On holy days, this number sometimes reached two thousand.

Douay, Liége, Bruges, and Saint Omer were the only cities of the Belgian Province, where the

---

[1] Litt. Ann. 1585, p. 347; H. S. 1581, 180.
[2] Litt. Ann. 1584. Coll. Audomar.

work of the sodalities could be established before receiving its definite organization by the decree of Gregory XIII. But by the restoration of religious peace, and by the zeal of Costerus, who had again become Provincial of Belgium in 1585, we shall soon see it spread rapidly in all the colleges of that country, and contribute most successfully to the honor of the Mother of God, and to the preservation of the Catholic religion.

To enumerate all the sodalities which were founded before 1584, in different parts of the world would take long, and would offer little interest. Let us name a few, which excite our attention on account of the illustrious persons whose names are connected with their origin. One was organized about 1575, among the students of Prague; it had for its first director the venerable Edmund Campian, who ten years later adorned the annals of the church in England with his glorious martyrdom.[1] The celebrated Maldonatus founded two at the college of Pont-à-Mousson, in Lorraine.[2] That of Naples was established in 1576 by Claudius Aquaviva, then rector.[3] At Milan, the Swiss college, which had Saint Charles Borromeo for its founder, welcomed the pious association, and by a bull of

---

[1] Historia prov. Austriacæ, auctore Socherio, p. 200.
[2] H. S. 1579, 43.   [3] Ibid. 1576, 47, 59.

March 25, 1580, the Sovereign Pontiff, on the petition of the holy Archbishop, granted special indulgences to the scholars who had been enrolled. He said that it was his wish to encourage in this way the godly deeds and the pious exercises of these meetings, and to help the young men to gather more abundant spiritual fruit for the salvation of their souls.[1] Saint Charles, and after him Cardinal Frederick, his nephew and his successor in the see of Milan, ever showed a lively interest in the work of the sodalities.

Everywhere the same spirit animated them — the spirit of zeal to vindicate devotion to Mary against the outrages of the Protestants, and the spirit of fervor, and of emulation in study and in literary progress. At Cologne, in 1581, the members of the sodality represented, in the form of a drama, the story of Saint Cecilia; and while some prominent citizens encouraged their attempts by paying the expenses of the representation, others, edified by the spectacle of Christian charity of which they had been witnesses, invited twelve poor students to their table, and furnished them with new suits of clothes. At Trèves, the four sodalities of the students divided among themselves the feasts of the Blessed Virgin, in order to

---

[1] We give this unpublished bull, *Salvatoris et Domini*, in an appendix.

honor the patroness of their studies, the Seat of Wisdom, by discourses, poems, and sometimes by dialogues of their own composition.[1] At Innspruck, the sodalists in spite of the opposition of certain timid Catholics, introduced the singing of the litany of Loretto in the churches: the Bishop, the Nuncio, and the Archduke encouraged their zeal for the public devotion to the Mother of God.[2] At Würzburg in a single year they recalled twenty heretics to Catholicity, and more than two hundred of the faithful to the frequenting of the sacraments.[3] At the college of Vienna, the society of Saint Barbara, honored fifteen years before by the virtues of the angelic Stanislaus Kostka, united itself in 1581 to the sodality of the Blessed Virgin.[4] The governor of the city, several senators and magistrates, allowed themselves to be persuaded by the exhortations and the examples of the members, publicly to issue the profession of the Catholic faith; three apostolic legates, passing through Vienna, inscribed themselves on the rolls of this sodality; the Empress and the Queen-Mother of France, not being able to be admitted to the

---

[1] Litt. Ann. 1581. Coll. Trevir. p. 175.
[2] Litt. Ann. 1581. Coll. Œnipont. 192.
[3] Ibid. Coll. Herbipolense, p. 178.
[4] It had been founded in 1579. Engstler: Brevis notitia de Sodalitate B. V. Assumptæ, Viennæ, anno 1579 erecta.

meetings of the pious associates, asked at least the favor of being counted among the Children of Mary.[1] The branch which flourished in Avignon, in 1577 devoted itself generously to the service of those stricken with the plague, and acted as substitutes for the Jesuits, who had seen eleven of their number succumb in the exercise of charity.[2] That of Lyons, quite prosperous in 1581, signalized itself by the practice of works of mercy towards prisoners and the sick.[3]

The details which we have just given of the first twenty years of the sodalities, will lead us to understand, much better than a general view, the influence of this salutary institution. In the midst of the relaxation in faith and morals which had invaded some Catholic nations, and in the face of the dangers with which the hatred of sectarians threatened the religion of our fathers, the sodalities of the Blessed Virgin helped powerfully to sustain works of faith and of charity, and to bring together and to unite the faithful; but the greatest service which they rendered was to renew the Christian generation, by strengthening the young in piety and in virtue, under the protection of the glorious Mother of God.

[1] Litt. Ann. Coll. Viennense, p. 196.
[2] H. S. 1577, 120.
[3] Litt. Ann. Coll. Lugdun. 1582, p. 163.

APPENDIX

Bull of Gregory XIII. Granting Special Indulgences to the Sodality of Milan, on the Petition of St. Charles Borromeo

Gregorius Papa XIII. ad perpetuam rei memoriam.

SALVATORIS et Domini Nostri JESU CHRISTI, qui ineffabili suæ charitatis abundantia antiqui hominis lapsum per immaculati corporis sui voluntarium in ara crucis sacrificium expiare dignatus est, vices licet immeriti gerentes in terris, gregem dominicum curæ nostræ commissum et ad devotionis sinceritatem et cordis contritionem peramplius augendam et confessionis et sacrosanctæ Eucharistiæ sacramentorum participationem, necnon aliorum charitatis et pietatis salutarium operum exercitium et escam spiritualium alimentorum, indulgentiis videlicet et peccatorum remissionibus libenter invitamus, ut exinde suorum abolita macula delictorum, præmissæ expiationis fructum facilius consequi et ad æternæ salutis gaudia feliciter pervenire mereantur.

Cum itaque, sicut accepimus, in collegio helvetico Helvetiorum et Rhætorum in domo S. Spiritus, Mediolani erecto, quædam scholarium congregationes sub titulo ac protectione Beatæ Mariæ Virginis cum institutæ vel instituendæ sint ad spiritualem vitam promovendam, Nos cupientes ut ipsi scholares salutaribus operibus et exercitiis eo ferventius intendant, quomodo exinde pro animarum suarum salute majora spiritualia dona adipisci posse agnoverint: precibus quoque dilecti filii nostri Caroli sanctæ Praxedis tituli, presbyteri cardinalis ecclesiæ Mediolani præsulis, nobis super hæc humiliter porrectis, inclinati, de Omnipotentis, Dei misericordia ac beatorum Apostolorum Petri et Pauli auctoritate confisi

Omnibus et singulis scholaribus et aliis fidelibus dicti Helveticorum collegii, qui alicui dictarum congregationum pro tempore se adscribi fecerint, die primi ingressus quem sacra peccatorum confessio et sacrosanctæ Eucharistiæ sumptio comitabitur, plenariam

Necnon illis qui jam in dictas congregationes cooptati sunt, quoquo die post notitiam habitam præsentium litterarum, pœnitentes et confessi sanctissimamque Eucharistiam sumpserint, pariter etiam plenariam omnium peccatorum suorum indulgentiam ac remissionem misericorditer in Domino concedimus.

Præterea quoties ex congregationis instituto simul congregati collationibus, colloquiis spiritualibus aut lectionibus sacris, adhortationibusque aut aliis piis exercitationibus per semihoræ spatium vacaverint, aut ad canendas litanias aut recitandam antiphonam B. Mariæ Virginis Salve Regina vel aliam pro temporis ratione, centum dierum.

Quoties vero examen conscientiæ agent, futuræ meditationis argumentum accipient aut rationem peractæ meditationis confessario aut præfecto spirituali reddent, unius anni.

Quoties coronam recitaverint qui consueverunt saltem singulis sabathis et vigiliis festorum B. Mariæ Virginis eam recitare, etiam unius anni.

Quoties pro fratre defuncto ex instituto congregationis orabunt, trium annorum.

Quoties peccata confitebuntur et sanctissimam Eucharistiam sumpserint, septem annorum.

Iis vero qui consueverint decimo quinto quoque die peccata confiteri et prima quaque mensis dominica et præterea in omnibus diebus festis Domini Nostri JESU CHRISTI, gloriosissimæ Virginis Mariæ, sanctorum Apostolorum, sancti Joannis Baptistæ, omniumque Sanctorum et S. Ambrosii, sacratissimam Eucharistiam sumere, — quoties id egerint, quindecim annorum indulgentiam.

At vero in festis diebus ejusdem B. Mariæ Virginis, tum in festo præcipuo Ecclesiæ collegii

Helvetiorum ac Rhætorum hujusmodi, si etiam præcedenti die jejunaverint, etiam plenariam.

Necnon in cujuslibet confratrum mortis articulo nomen JESUS et Mariæ, corde si minus voce potuerint, implorando, plenariam pariter omnium peccatorum suorum indulgentiam ac remissionem misericorditer in Domino concedimus et elargimur.

Contrariis non obstantibus quibuscumque præsentibus, perpetuis futuris temporibus valituris.

Datum Romæ apud S. Petrum sub annulo piscatoris die XXV martii MDLXXX, pontificatus nostri anno 8°.

Quarto calendas Julii MDLXXXIV requisitus Illustrissimus et Reverendissimus Carolus Borromeus Cardinalis Tituli S⁂ Praxedis qualis dies primus ingressus, cujus indulgentiæ mentio fit, dicendus esset et habendus, declaravit esse illum diem, quo primo post confirmationem, sodalitatem ingreditur, qui receptus fuerit.

Book II

The Sodalities from 1584 to the Suppression of the Society of Jesus in 1773

CHAPTER I

Canonical Institution of the Work of the Sodalities

THE various sodalities which we have seen established were inspired with a common desire to develop devotion to the Blessed Virgin, principally in the colleges, and, by this means, to form the young to a Christian life and to solid piety. Progress in studies, the exercise of charity and zeal against the errors of the times, entered equally, according to circumstances, into the proper character of these associations. Nevertheless, outside of this community of views and of these pious practices, there was no bond of union. Although some, like those of Douay, of Sienna, and of Madrid, had been established conformably to the rules of the sodality of Rome, the greater number had been formed independently. Others — those of Cologne and of Paris, for instance — had obtained a pontifical or episcopal approbation and particular indulgences. Several, too far from Rome, had been unable to have recourse to the Sovereign Pontiff to obtain the desired indulgences, and the majority remained deprived of the spiritual favors granted by Gregory XIII. to the sodality of the Roman College.

At Rome, a union, or rather the most complete unity, had been maintained among the various sodalities; they were considered as so many sections of the original sodality, which was called the *Primary Sodality*.[1] Besides insuring the common enjoyment of numerous indulgences, the unity maintained a uniformity of aim and of direction, and proved an element of vitality. V. R. F. Claudius Aquaviva, elected General of the Jesuits in 1581, was foremost in appreciating these advantages. He wished that all the associations already established independently of that of Rome, might be formed into a vast network, of which all the threads would converge to the same centre, — a combination that would insure them the stability and the strength of which their isolation would have deprived them. He exposed,

---

[1] H. S. 1584, 15.

therefore, to the Sovereign Pontiff, the difficulties that the different sodalities met with, obliged as they were to address themselves, each one in particular, to the Roman Court, in order to draw upon the treasury of indulgences: and he showed the advantages which they could reap from an organization which would unite them intimately to the *Primary Sodality* of Rome. Gregory XIII. approved of this plan, and expressed the hope that from the Roman College, which he had so generously founded, piety and devotion to Mary, as well as the sacred and the profane sciences, might spread throughout the entire world. He therefore signed, on the 5th of December, 1584, the bull *Omnipotentis Dei*, by which he established the sodality of the Roman College as the centre of all the others, and granted a canonical existence, and the pontifical approbation to all those who might enter into this grand union. We subjoin the translation of this bull,[1] so important for the future of the work.

Gregory, Bishop, Servant of the Servants of God,
IN PERPETUAL REMEMBRANCE.

"In accordance with the example of our Saviour, God Omnipotent, Who from the overflowing

---

[1] Bourassé, Summa Aurea de Laudibus B. M. V., Vol. VII. Bullarium Marianum, p. 100. — Instit. Soc. Jesu. Pragæ, p. 82.

of His mercy continually pours into the hearts of His faithful the grace of divine inspirations and the fervor of devotion, and in order that these His servants may render His majesty due homage with fruit to themselves, and that they may cultivate all works of piety, We interest ourselves, as, indeed, it is the duty of Our pastoral charge, in favoring them in the performance of these works and of godly exercises, so that their piety and devotion may meet with constant increase, and that they themselves may reach in security the goal of salvation.

"Before this We had been apprised that the greater part of the good and devout youths who are engaged in the study of letters in Our Roman College of the Society of Jesus, moved by a keen sentiment of affection for the Blessed Virgin Mary, Mother of God, and urged by the pious exhortations of their teachers, had formed the practice of visiting on certain days and at fixed hours the Church of the Annunciation attached to their college, for the purpose of purifying their consciences with sincere devotion and with lively sorrow by means of confession and holy communion, of reciting the divine office, of listening to instructions and conferences, and of performing other salutary works of the spirit, and that, thanks to their example, many others of the faithful had become united and associated for the same objects of Christian zeal. Therefore, desirous of giving further development to these pious associations, we had granted to the students, and to the rest of the faithful who take up the practice of these holy works and pious exercises, many indulgences and remissions of penalties, as may be witnessed at fuller length in the letters which We issued on that occasion.

"Since then — as Our well-beloved son, the General of the Society of Jesus, has recently represented to Us — as the colleges of the same society have been multiplied in the various parts of the world, and especially in the principal cities of Europe, for the purpose of forming youth in virtue and morality, and of imbuing them with true piety and sound doctrine, and as the day-scholars who flock thither for instruction have evinced great fervor in imitating these excellent works of piety, and as there has thence been reaped a copious harvest for the glory of God, for the veneration of the ever-blessed Virgin, for the welfare of the people and the consolation of souls, intent as We are upon warmly cherishing and securely maintaining this praiseworthy zeal for good works and devout exercises, it hath seemed good to Us that the Roman College (the new and magnificent building of which is now being erected at Our expense and under Our auspices), after having originated these pious and salutary exercises, should possess the first and principal sodality canonically established. We would thus fulfil the humble petition of the General of the society, who has entreated Us to give Our approbation to this work and of Our Apostolic benevolence, to provide for it as We may deem it to be opportune.

"Wishing, then, most cordially to second the pious desires of the students, and to encourage their ardor in the performance of these exercises of devotion, We accede to his prayer, and by Our Apostolic authority, and by the tenor of this present brief, We erect and We institute in the church designated above a sodality which shall be the primary, and shall be the mother of all the others, with the title of the Annunciation of the Blessed Virgin Mary, composed of the day-scholars of the aforesaid college, and of all the other faithful devoted to that society, desiring that it shall be directed by the General aforesaid and each of his successors, and after their death and until the canonical election of a new General, by the Vicar of the society, without, however, prejudicing the interests of this society. And in order that the members of this sodality may always receive increase of devotion and of piety in the graces and heavenly gifts with which it will be favored, trusting in the mercy of God Omnipotent, by the authority of the blessed apostles Peter and Paul, We freely grant in the Lord, by the tenor of this present brief, and by Our Apostolic authority, a plenary indulgence of all their sins, on the day of their reception, to all and each of the faithful who are truly penitent and have confessed their sins, and who shall thenceforth rank as members of this pious sodality, and on that day shall have received the most Holy Sacrament of the Eucharist in that church or in any other whatsoever. We also grant them a similar indulgence when at the point of death." . . .

Then follows the enumeration of the indulgences which the Sovereign Pontiff attached to the various works proper to the sodality. This we omit, with the passing remark that the works of mercy become traditional amongst the members of the sodalities, were not forgotten in the list. Thus Gregory XIII. granted a year of indulgence for all visits to the sick, either members of the sodalities or others, at their homes or at the hospital; for presence at holy mass or at funerals, and for the reconciliation of enemies.

In this brief one only sodality is recognized by the Holy See. It is that of the Annunciation, established in the church of the Roman College, and bearing the title of the Primary Sodality. The General of the Society of Jesus, who has the supreme direction of it, receives full power to affiliate other confraternities to it, and, by the very fact of their affiliation, they gain a canonical existence and all the favors granted to the Primary Sodality. It is required, however, by the terms of this bull, that they should be erected under the common title of the Annunciation, and remain under the control of the General of the Jesuits. From this arose the custom of sending to new organizations a diploma, in which he recognized them as constituting one and the same sodality with that of the Roman College.

It is from the year 1584, when its official existence commenced, that the Roman Sodality of the Annunciation dates its origin; hence it chose this year as a starting-point in reckoning its first two centennial jubilees.[1]

[1] Esposizione delle regole della Congregazione prima primaria. Rome, Bourlié, 1821, p. 4.

CHAPTER II

Development and Organization of the Sodalities

THE work so modestly begun twenty years before, and now placed on a firm footing, was destined to grow into a vast association of prayer and effort, having its centre in Rome, and extending even to the smallest colleges of the society. Ere long it was to gain still wider scope, and beyond the narrow limits of collegiate institutions it was to exercise its influence over all ages and all conditions of society.

In the Roman College, the Primary Association was soon divided into three sections; the first was reserved for students of philosophy and theology who had already completed their twentieth year; the second was composed of those who were from fourteen to twenty years old ; the third included the younger pupils. This is the origin of the well-known name of *Prima Primaria*, or first primary, borne by the principal sodality, and appearing even in the inscription over the entrance of its first place of meeting : —

PRIMA · PRIMARIA
CONGREGATIO
OMNIVM · CONGREGATIONVM
TOTO · ORBE · DIFFVSARVM
MATER · ET · CAPVT.[1]

The bull *Omnipotentis Dei* did not limit the work of the sodalities to young students. Very naturally the graduates of the Roman College wished to continue to enjoy the advantages of the sodality and to take part in its reunions;[2] it was judged more prudent, however, to erect new sodalities, whose direction might be adapted to the special requirements of their members. In the meanwhile, several associations had been formed outside of Rome, under the protection of the Holy Virgin, but not bearing the title of the Annunciation. Some of these were designed for men of the world. From this time, others were founded for all conditions of society, for priests, for the nobility, for the middle classes, for artisans, and even for peasants. Everywhere recourse was had to the power of the sodality as a means of confirming the faith of Catholics against the

[1] Translation : — The First Primary Sodality, the Mother and Head of all the Sodalities spread over the Whole Earth.
[2] H. S. 1587, 3.

seductions and errors of the time. Even more was expected from the associations of men of mature age than from those of the young, on account of the natural inconstancy of youth.[1] This state of affairs caused V. R. F. Claudius Aquaviva to solicit a new favor from Pope Sixtus V., the successor of Gregory XIII.

He represented to the Sovereign Pontiff that the number of the associates and the diversity of their needs, had often made it necessary to establish several sodalities in the same city, and that even before the bull of Gregory XIII., some pious men living in the world had formed others, which were wholly distinct from those of the students. On the one hand, F. Aquaviva desired that these sodalities should keep their own titles as a distinguishing mark, but on the other he wished them to be affiliated to the Primary Sodality of Rome, that they might participate in the favors granted to the sodalities of the Annunciation. Sixtus V. acceded to all his requests by the bull *Superna dispositione*, dated Jan. 5, 1586,[2] which he confirmed the following year by the bull *Romanum decet Pontificem*.[3] In the sequel a series of pontifical rescripts was to extend still further the powers of the General of the Society of Jesus.

[1] H. S. 1587, 4.   [2] *Summa aurea*, vol. VII. p. 123.
[3] 29 September 1587. Instit. Soc. Jesu, Pragæ, p. 99.

Instead of transcribing them here, we will give merely their substance. Not satisfied with confirming in their whole extent the privileges already granted, the Sovereign Pontiffs, Clement VIII. (1602), and Gregory XV. (1621) authorized the General to establish sodalities in all the houses of the Society, including simple residences, and even to confer the privileges of affiliation upon all such as should be established elsewhere with the approbation of the Ordinary. They also settled the principle that the different names they might bear should form no obstacle to their union with the Prima Primaria. This decision revoked, in favor of the sodalities, all previous bulls which had prohibited a similar communication of favors designated by the phrase *ad instar*.[1]

As early as 1585, Claudius Aquaviva notified the Provincials of the Society of the favors granted by Gregory XIII., and indicated to them the formalities to be observed in erecting sodalities of the Blessed Virgin. He now communicated to

---

[1] Clement VIII. *Cum sicut nobis*. ... 30 Aug. 1602, ... nonobstantibus nostra de non concedendis indulgentiis ad instar, aliisque constitutionibus et ordinationibus apostolicis, cæterisque contrariis quibuscumque. — Greg. XV. *Alias pro parte*. ... 15 April, 1621 ... decernentes prædictas Gregorii et Sixti prædecessorum necnon præsentes litteras, sub constitutione recentis memoriæ Clementis VIII., super modo et forma confraternitatis erigendi, aggregandi edita, minime comprehendi.

them the substance of the briefs of Sixtus V. and Clement VIII. He also caused to be inserted in the Institute of his Order, among the Ordinances for Generals,[1] certain specifications of which the following are a summary: 1st. Every sodality which may desire to be aggregated to the Primary Sodality, must send two copies of its application, — one addressed to the General of the Society, the other to the prefect and assistants of the Primary Sodality. 2d. The expenses of this aggregation are to be borne, not by the sodality of the Roman College, but by those which ask the favor. 3d. The sodalities, as such, can possess no real estate or fixed revenues.

These details of organization were the result of experience. Already some associates in Valencia and Naples had proposed to settle annual revenues upon their establishments; but Aquiviva prudently ordered that their offers should be refused, as he did not wish the sodalities to become transformed into confraternities, and so lose the privilege of exemption, according to the terms of the bull of Clement VIII., entitled *Quæcumque a sede apostolica*.[2] Many times afterwards, the Generals renewed the orders of Aquaviva upon

[1] *Institutum Soc. Jesu*, Ordinationes Præpos. Generalium, cap. XXI., 2, 3.
[2] H. S. 1587, 4-5.

this point. In some cities the sodalities desired to found *monts de piété*. This was only permitted on condition that individual members should take the management of them, using only their own names and bringing no responsibility upon the association.[1]

In addition to this general organization, were there any special rules common to all the sodalities and *prescribing* in detail any works of devotion or charity? None at all; a spirit of breadth and foresight had presided over the definitive establishment of these associations. After pointing out their character, aim, and essential elements, the superiors left to the prudence of their directors the arrangement of minor points, according to the circumstances and necessities of time and place. The first rules of the *Annunziata*[2] were

---

[1] *Responsa Præpositorum Generalium ad Varios Superiores, Collecta in Provincia Flandro-Belgica.* § 10. De Congregationibus. Congregationes sub cura Societatis non possunt fundare montem misericordiæ a se dependentem, quia si haberent ejusmodi bona, ab episcopis possent visitari. (12 nov. 1594, ad prov. Neapol.) — Ut assignati reditus teneri possint, potest institui alius cœtus extra septa nostra, in quem non admittantur nisi qui sunt ex congregatione nostra, cui committantur reditus et curæ alienæ a congregationibus nostris. (28 aug. 1610, ad prov. Austriac.) — Nec etiam jus ad certas eleemosynas habere potest congregatio; quæ si dentur, accipi possunt, s non dentur, non possunt peti tanquam ex justitia debitæ. (1616, ad prov. Sard.)

[2] *Manuale Sodalita is B. M. V.*, collectum olim a Sodalitate

expressed in these terms: "Since the members make profession of a more perfect life, they are *invited* to devote themselves with more than ordinary zeal to works of Christian piety, such as frequent confession and communion, daily recitation of the Rosary or of the Office of the Blessed Virgin, meditation, visitation of prisons and hospitals, catechetical instruction of the ignorant, and other Christian works of this kind; they may engage in these occupations singly according to their circumstances or their devotion, or the whole sodality may unite in them as a body; in this they will follow the advice of their father director and of the superior of the college." It is but the aim and the general spirit of the sodalities which are manifested by the rules, while they leave the settlement of details to the discretion of the directors; and, as might be expected, even a cursory examination of the manuals of sodalities belonging to the seventeenth and eighteenth centuries, reveals great diversity in the secondary regulations. This was inevitable, especially after the work was no longer bounded by the limits of colleges, but had been extended among all conditions and classes of society. The direction to be given

---

Leodiensi. Mussiponti, 1608. Pars 2da: Leges Congregationum. ... According to Father Ribadenaira (*Catalogus Scriptorum S. J.*) Father Delrio edited the first edition that had appeared at Liége.

to a reunion of cultivated men must necessarily differ from that which would be suited to a confraternity of laborers. It will, however, be readily understood that the Directors conformed as far as possible to the rules of the Primary Sodality, with reference to prayers and other devotional exercises, which might be used in common by all classes of associates.

A question of some interest here suggests itself: Did the rules of the Primary Sodality of Rome prescribe at least a common formula, a precisely similar act of consecration, for all who entered the different sodalities of the Blessed Virgin? We have seen that the formula in use at the present day in Belgium, dates from the earliest times, and that its identical terms are to be found in the Manual of Father Costerus.[1] In 1694, Father Crasset gave it as in general use in the sodalities

---

[1] This formula is found together with others in the *Leges et Statuta Congregationis B. V.* Monachii, an. MDCIII., p. 62; in the *Règles de la Sodalité . . . approuvée en Anvers entre les nations l'an* 1610 *sous le titre de l'Immaculée Conception . . .* chez Jean Cnobbaert; in the *Sodalis Parthenicus* published at Luxemburg by Kleber, 1758, in the chapter: Leges ex romano exemplari paucis comprehensæ. A commentary on it may be found in Stengel, S. J.: *Exegesis super Sacramenti Mariani formula*, Ingolstadt, 12mo, 1620; in Frölich, S. J.: *Sermones ad Sodales Parthenicos.* Dillingen, 1709; Nadasi, *Annales Mariani*, n. 513, seems to know no other: "ea qua nos B. Virgini dedicamus, formula: Sancta Maria, mater Dei, etc."

of France; he adds, however, that there is room for doubt as to whether it is the most ancient. "It appears from our books," says he, "that this prayer is not the original form of consecration to the Blessed Virgin, but is only an abridgment of a longer formula, which was still in use within the last sixty years." He then gives this earlier act of consecration as it was preserved in the Professed House of the Society in Paris, signed by Cardinal de la Rochefoucauld and other associates. In fact, the last edition of the *Leges et Statuta Sodalitatum;* published at Rome in 1855, which is an authority for the traditions of the Prima Primaria, gives no other formula. It seems, on the whole, most probable that the sodalities of Belgium and Germany faithfully retained the formula bequeathed to them by Costerus, while the sodality of Rome adopted, from the first, the one which Father Crasset afterwards found in the archives of the Professed House, at Paris.

We will look no further into the canonical organization of the sodalities. Additional details, which we might furnish, would occupy too much space, and would likewise trench upon the domain of writers on Canon Law.

CHAPTER III

Extension of the Work of the Sodalities, especially in the Belgian Provinces

THE encouragement and spiritual favors which Popes Gregory XIII. and Sixtus V. had bestowed so liberally on the members of the sodalities, gave a magnificent impulse to devotion toward Our Lady. The sodalities which, under various titles, had been established for several years in a great number of cities, solicited the advantages of affiliation, and solemnly celebrated their union with that of the Roman College. In the short space of two years, one hundred and thirty-nine certificates of aggregation were forwarded to different parts of the Catholic world.[1]

Titles in the greatest variety, testifying to the confidence of the faithful of all countries in the protection of the Mother of God, pressed for enrolment upon the registers of the Prima Primaria. Here, the members had chosen the title of "Our Lady of the Rosary," in memory of the earlier

---
[1] Litt. Ann. 1589. Col. Rom.

connection with the celebrated confraternity of the Dominicans; there, the patroness was "Our Lady of the Angels," "Our Lady of Peace," or "of Succor;" elsewhere, again, it was the "Mother of Sorrows," the "Queen of Priests," "of Martyrs," or "of all Saints." Sometimes a title commemorated one of the mysteries of her life, while again she was invoked by the particular name of some miraculous shrine,[1] as Our Lady of Loretto, of Hungary, etc. Very many of the new sodalities took the same title with that of Rome.

At that time there was not one of the colleges of the Society (which numbered over two hundred at the beginning of the seventeenth century), in which the Blessed Virgin might not behold numerous gatherings of students wholly devoted to her honor, and to the faithful practice of their duties as Christians.

But no part of the world welcomed the sodalities with so much ardor as the Low Countries. Until 1585 the religious revolution had obstructed the action of the Society of Jesus. As soon as peace was restored, Father Costerus, who had been promoted a second time to the government of the Belgian province, employed himself, with all the ardor of his devotion, in establishing this work of

[1] Nadasi has taken pains to collect them in 1658: *Annales Mariani*, p. 635, 638.

the children of Mary. Bruges, Ypres, Anvers, Mons,[1] and several other cities where the liberality of the Duke of Parma opened colleges for the Society, saw the sodalities inaugurated at the same time. The Reformation had everywhere attacked devotion to Mary, and Costerus exerted himself to implant it everywhere in the hearts of the young. Wherever it was possible, he took pains to found sodalities of influential men in her honor.

At Anvers he established, on the eighth of December, 1585, a branch, the zeal of which deserves special mention. In this city, where Mary had reigned as a sovereign from time immemorial, the iconoclastic sectaries had signalized their hatred by criminal profanations. Her pious votaries were now ambitious of re-establishing their Patroness in her rights by a public and, in a manner, official act of homage. They obtained permission to place her statue in front of the city hall, and 'to invest it with a crown and sceptre in presence of the new magistrates, as an acknowledgment of her power and of the protection she had always granted to the commercial capital. This ceremony was celebrated with a magnificence which rejoiced the hearts of all good citizens, and gave complete satisfaction to the ardent propagator of devotion to Mary.[2]

---

[1] H. S., 1584, n. 99, 1585, n. 127, 1586, n. 55.
[2] Précis Historiques, Mai, 1882.

At Louvain, which was a prey to the discussions raised by the errors of Baïus, it seemed to Costerus that a devotion traditional in the university might be efficacious in calming the minds of the disputants. And so, immediately after the publication of the bull, *Omnipotentis Dei*, he established a sodality among the students. He afterwards had the consolation of hearing that Lensæus de Bailleul, who had been among the foremost in the contest, had, in 1793, enrolled himself in the number of the associates. From Liége, Costerus wrote, on the 1st of January, 1589, to the general of the Society, to inform him of the success of the sodality, and of the great number of prominent men who were consecrating themselves to the service of the Blessed Virgin Mary.[1] Shortly after, one of the most celebrated writers of the time, Justus Lipsius, entered the association, to sanctify in it the last years of his life; and, after him, names still more illustrious were to honor the sodalities of Louvain.

At Brussels the sodalities could not show names so glorious in the annals of science, yet Costerus had the happiness of seeing enrolled there men whose piety furnished a noble example. In the court of Albert and Isabella there was no want of fervent Catholics ready to make open profession

[1] Archives du Royaume de B:lgique, bound MS., vol. I., n. 772.

of their love for Mary. In 1617 the Latin sodality included a score of members of the Privy Council, and of the Chancery of Brabant. The Duke of Neubourg, also, who had recently been brought back from Protestantism to the religion of his ancestors, entered the body-guard of Mary. Brussels finally counted nineteen sodalities, of various ages and classes.

With what joy did the good old man see them gather by turns at the feet of that miraculous statue of Our Lady of Mercy, which had been transferred to the house of the Jesuits from the ancient chapel of St. Christopher, where it had become celebrated, and which has always, even in our own day, received such marked veneration from the faithful.[1]

It was at Brussels that he was to end his long career, which had been so fruitful in the works of eternal life. While he was Provincial, and afterwards during the thirty years which he had divided between preaching and the composition of numerous works, he had contributed much toward repairing the ruin of religion in his country. Under the protection of her who has triumphed

---

[1] In 1854 it was crowned in the name of the Sovereign Pontiff, with a most brilliant ceremonial on the part of the army and the court of Leopold II., in the church of Notre Dame de la Chapelle, where it had been placed in 1804.

over all heresies, he beheld the work so dear to his heart spreading in all directions; everywhere pious Catholics were boldly professing that devotion to Mary which had once been despised as childishness or detested as idolatry. The memory of Costerus long survived in the hearts of the sodalists of Germany and Belgium;[1] at the end of the last century the sodalities of Anvers commemorated by a jubilee the name of their first founder and his zeal against heresy.[2]

There are few countries where the devout soldiers of Mary have spread so widely and done such good service as in the Belgian provinces. Twenty years after the death of Costerus, ninety-eight sodalities existed there.

The sodalities of Bavaria were perhaps even more flourishing; but is it at all possible to establish a comparison? Have not all Catholic countries vied with one another in claiming the glory of an extraordinary zeal for the honor and service of the Mother of God? Wherever the Society of Jesus put forth its efforts to enlarge the kingdom

---

[1] He died on the sixth of December, 1619, in a happy old age, without a single cloud having been cast over his days by sin or sorrow. "The story of his life shall be told, for so noble a subject is well deserving of a book," wrote Father Bourghois, on learning his death. This prediction is still unverified; but why should it not tempt some pious servant of Mary?

[2] Précis Historiques. Mai, 1882.

of Jesus Christ, either by preaching or education, it seemed equally desirous of extending the sovereignty of the Blessed Mother of the Saviour. The principal means it employed, both in its own colleges and among those living in the world, was always the work of the sodalities.

Even in heathen countries, in the Chinese, Japanese, and American missions, the Society rallied new Christians round the standard of the Queen of Heaven. In 1664, eighty-seven years after China had opened her doors to the preaching of the gospel, the Christian religion, and, with it, devotion to Mary, had penetrated into ten provinces. More than four hundred sodalities had been formed there in honor of the Blessed Virgin or of the Passion of her Divine Son. Some of these included over a hundred members, chosen from among the most fervent converts. Zealous catechists were trained in them, and they doubtlessly had a large share in the work of conversions, the number of which rose at this period to five thousand or even six thousand a year.[1] The Sodality of the Mother of Mercy in Pekin furnished charitable assistance to indigent Christians.[2]

In Paraguay the Jesuit fathers had organized

---

[1] Fr. De Rougemont, *Historia Tartaro-Sinica*, Louvain, Hullegaerde, 1673, p. 193, n. 133.

[2] *H. S.* 1628, 221.

settlements of Christian Indians, or reservations, under the names of the Assumption, the Conception, Loretto, and other similar titles. In the bosom of these, chosen bands were gathered under the protection of Mary. Christian piety will not then be astonished at the words of a bishop of Buenos Ayres, Dom Pedro Faxardo, who said: " I do not believe that one mortal sin is committed in a year in the reservations." This is the highest eulogy ever bestowed on these Christian communities.

While the work was performing these wonders in barbarous countries, it had to struggle, in company with the Children of St. Ignatius, against the persecutions constantly fomented against devotion to Mary by the Protestants, who dreaded nothing so much as " the Popery and idolatry" of the Jesuits. On the other hand, the Jesuits, to preserve the faith of Catholics, were gathering them behind the ægis of Mary, and were sometimes able to protect even the temporal interests of the associates. At Augsburg, the Protestant bakers pitilessly expelled all Catholic bakers from their guild. They could gain no redress, as they were excluded by their faith from every privilege. But at the suggestion of a Jesuit, they obtained leave from the city council to form a sodality of their own, which enabled them

Extension of the Work

to maintain their ground against an odious monopoly.[1]

England, once the isle of Saints and "Our Lady's Dower," consecrated by more than one of her kings to the august Queen of Heaven,[2] did not pass through the troubled days of the Reform without receiving the new association upon her shores. It was established in a moment of sunshine, too soon followed by fresh tempests. At the end of the seventeenth century, F. Edward Scarisbrick, who preached at the court of Queen Henrietta Maria, and was afterwards chaplain of King James II., was Director of a sodality of the Immaculate Conception. He also edited a manual of rules for its use.[3] This sodality disappeared with the college of Savoy; but on the continent, in France, in Spain, in the Low Countries, numerous English colleges, supported by the generosity of the faithful, kept up prosperous and fervent sodalities.

---

[1] H. S. pars V., lib. XVI., 33.

[2] Waterton, *Pietas Mariana Britannica*, London, 1879, pp. 11-17.

[3] See De Backer, under Neuvill, Rules and Instructions for the Sodality of the Immaculate Conception of the most Glorious and Ever Virgin Mary Mother of God; with a short appendix relating to the second congregation of the same sodality, MDCCIII, 12⁰, 150 pp. This bibliographical note may perhaps contain the answer to the question proposed by Mr. Waterton, op. cit., p. 99, note 34.

In these, new apostles were preparing themselves to dispute with heresy the kingdom of the Virgin Mother. In an abridgment of the rules of the sodality of Saint Omer,[1] the young members profess it to be the object of their pious union, to promote true devotion to the Queen of Heaven, "that she may enjoy again full and peaceful possession of her ancient dowry."[2] Would that this hope might speedily be realized, nourished as it has been in the hearts of so many of that noble nation! The servants of Mary are not praying in vain for the conversion of England. In the further development of our subject we shall see how the sodality of Our Lady, almost everywhere suppressed at the same time with the Society of Jesus, was transplanted to flourish and produce blessed fruit beneath English skies.

We have now seen the work of Father Leonius approved and recognized by the supreme Head of Holy Church, and extended with the Society of Jesus to the utmost limits of the earth. It is time to look more closely at the good which it accomplished.

[1] An Abridgement of the Rules of the Sodality of our Blessed Lady under the Charge of the Society of Jesus at Saint Omer's, 1726.

[2] "Of her ancient dowry," see Waterton, op. cit. p. 17.

CHAPTER IV

The Sodalities in the Colleges

IT was in the colleges that the sodalities took their rise, and it is there that we should first study them and ascertain their influence upon Christian education. It is shown by experience that young people feel the influence of their companions more readily than that of their teachers. It is difficult for masters to divest themselves altogether of an air of authority in their intercourse with their pupils. But authority often arouses prejudice; it presents itself to the mind of the young man with a more or less repulsive aspect; he is unwilling to submit to its weight or allow himself to be moulded by it. Far more efficacious is a good example or a wholesome word coming from an equal. His companions leave him free play — liberty to act or not as he pleases; they do not pretend to impose their own course upon him as a rule, or even to offer it as a model. And in this way he is the more easily persuaded, and adopts their line of conduct without fully realizing the impulse which he obeys. Is it not, then, an element of success in education to profit by this natural tendency of youth, and to give pupils an opportunity of guiding one another in the right way?

It was one of the best features of the sodalities that they helped to form, in the colleges, a nucleus of young men penetrated with a spirit of piety, and a love of duty, and generously devoted to all that constitutes the strength and beauty of the Christian life. Though they were numerous enough to counteract the influence of any unsuitable members, they were carefully chosen and thoroughly tried, with the view of forming a select troop, more worthy of praise for quality than numbers. Besides, they aspired to an aim too lofty to be consistent with indiscriminate admission into their ranks. While the majority of men are satisfied with fulfilling what duty absolutely exacts, the clients of Mary vied with each other in zealous imitation of their heavenly patroness; guided by the sentiment of love rather than by fear, they aimed at perfection, at that holiness of Christian life realized in the most perfect of creatures.

Such was the spirit of the sodalities. "It is desired," says the first of the general rules, "that the associates should be distinguished for their devotion to Mary; that they should strive by a pure and irreproachable conduct to copy in their own lives the eminent virtues of which she has given them the example; that, animating one another in her love and service, they should endeavor to kindle in their hearts an ardent desire of increasing the glory of her holy name."

The influence of the members of the sodalities upon their fellow-pupils was due to two causes: first, their virtue and eminent piety won for them respect and consideration, and besides, they usually distinguished themselves in their studies. But talent and merit inspire no less esteem in college life than in the world. The history of the Jesuit colleges offers frequent examples of the superiority of the associates over their companions in the same classes. It is stated in the *Lettres Annuelles*, that at Mayence, and at Pont-à-Mousson [1] they took all the prizes, and the writer adds that the same thing frequently happened in the other colleges. Numerous cases are mentioned where young students, under the protection of the Blessed Virgin, gained unexpected successes, and where talents, long dormant, had been aroused to a remarkable development.[2] Such is the natural fruit of piety. One great advantage which it secures is that, by withdrawing youthful

---

[1] Litt. Ann. 1589, Mogunt. 1596 Mussipontan. et passim.
[2] Ibid. 1594, Herbipol, 1600, Mclshem. 1613, Biturigense Coll.

minds from vice and from dangerous interests, it gives them that repose and serenity which are indispensable for study. And again, by disciplining the will to overcome frivolity and inattention, it renders the mind capable of more concentrated and fruitful effort.

From their origin in the Roman College, the sodalities, as we have seen, had a practical object, secondary, it is true, to their principal end, but closely connected with it. This was advancement in study. In persuance of it, literary reunions were established. In these modest circles, formed everywhere in accordance with the *Ratio Studiorum*, the members stimulated one another, and sometimes produced literary compositions that cost much labor, while at other times they exercised themselves in improvisation, criticism, or discussion. These academic labors were usually, if not always, employed upon religious or pious subjects, as the praises of the Blessed Virgin. The dramas which they produced in public on some special occasions, were usually of a religious character. The plot was often some mystery in the life of our Saviour, or perhaps a remarkable fact in the history of the Church, or an edifying incident in the career of some Saint.[1]

---

[1] We subjoin the titles of a series of dramas played at the College of Anvers, according to the manuscript history of that institution;

The college sodalities, besides furnishing an element of education, favored works of zeal and Christian charity. We have given proofs of this in regard to the first sodality of the Roman College. It would be easy to multiply them, and to show how associates of the upper classes assisted according to their opportunities in the religious instruction of poor children in the cities and villages. In many colleges, catechetical work was organized. In Rome,[1] for example, they went about the streets on holidays, and gathered the unemployed people in squares, to instruct them in the truths of faith. Others brought ignorant children to church to teach them the catechism, and the secular priests gave a friendly reception to the youthful apostles. At Anvers, a sodality was formed among the pupils, having for its particular object the religious instruction of the ignorant.[2] The following are the simple terms in which the

---

Theodosius pœnitens, Sancta Barbara, Adolescens impœnitens, Sancta Elisabeth, regina Hungariæ; Jonas, Sanctus Aloysius, Sanctus Franciscus Borgia, Isaac Angelus, Sanctus Ignatius, Sanctus Ambrosius, Sapor, rex Persarum, Mordochœus, Sinica persecutio. The *Theatrum Solitudinis Asceticæ* of Father Lang and the *Theatrum Asceticum* of Father Neumayr, and of Father Gachet, give us a very edifying idea of these pious representations. (Cf. DE BACKER, *Bibliothèque des Écrivains S. J.*)

[1] *Lit. Ann.* 1596, Coll. Rom.
[2] *Précis historiques*, Mai, 1882.

young supporters of this work expressed its purpose; they are drawn from the register, which is still preserved in the Jesuit College: "In taking our walks, we have often noticed that among the country children there reigned, instead of the fear of the Lord, great disorder, a habit of blasphemy, and a deplorable ignorance of the divine precepts . . . As members of the Sodality of the Blessed Virgin, and so, anxious to improve every occasion of doing a good work in her honor, we decided sometimes to go to instruct these children, and teach very simply — which is all we can do — what a Christian needs to know for his own salvation : — the whole in honor of God, and of our Patroness the Blessed Virgin Mary." Under the direction of a zealous and prudent master, nothing is impossible to generous-minded youth. The sodality of the young catechists of Anvers continued its operations, even after regular preparation for first communion was established in that city, through the efforts of the Jesuits and of the secular priests.

The number of cities where the young students interested themselves in catechising poor children, is considerable. This will seem less strange if we remember that, in the seventeenth century, preparation for first communion was not made with as much care as the clergy bestow upon it at present.

The custom of making the occasion itself a public solemnity is of comparatively recent date.[1]

It is easy to imagine how these humble manifestations of zeal would strengthen the piety of the students and develop the germs of an apostolic vocation. According to the testimony of Pope Benedict XIV., who had himself belonged to the sodality of the Roman College, "a great number of young men in the sodalities, thanks to the affectionate devotion they had early conceived for the Mother of God, rose to the most sublime degrees of charity. Some, generously abandoning the perishable goods and pleasures of this world, sought a holier state of life, and gave themselves entirely to the work of their own perfection and the salvation of souls. Others, walking from their earliest years in the way of innocence and piety, under the protection of the Blessed Virgin Mary, have preserved to the end the blamelessness which befits a disciple of Jesus Christ, and a servant of Mary, and merited final perseverance as the crown of their good example."[2]

These words of Benedict XIV. have an especial application to certain sodalities which were formed in imitation of the one at Ingolstadt, established by the venerable Father Jacob Rem. The aim of

---

[1] Précis Hist., Avril, 1884.
[2] Bulla aurea: "Gloriosæ Dominæ."

this association was so elevated that a contemporary said, "It is not a man who conceived this work; it was inspired or dictated by an angel." Such a name was not wholly unsuited to the venerable Father himself, so angelic was the purity of his life, which had never been stained by mortal sin. To gain a conception of the loftiness of this work, let us try to trace the idea of it, as it must have been formed in the heart of the holy priest.

As it came from the hand of God, all creation bore the stamp of the divine beauty, and God found it worthy of His omnipotence. He proclaimed that it was good. But in this creation there arose a monster alien to God, and ready to annihilate Him, if it were possible. God must repel and hate this enemy as much as He loves the work of His own hands. This monster is evil; it is sin, the source of all the disorders and all the ills which have rushed like a torrent over humanity. Since its irruption the world has been like an invaded kingdom, like a violated sanctuary.

Sin has obscured the work of God, as sombre night veils the firmament. But, as brilliant stars delight our eyes in the midst of the darkness, so from this overclouded earth shine forth, in the sight of God, some pure souls, who, by virtue of the redemption, have rent off the gloomy veil of sin, and sparkle with the rays of sanctifying grace. On them the divine glance rests with joy. They alone are pleasing to the Creator, and for their sake He delays to punish the abomination of sin in the masses of mankind, as He would have spared guilty Sodom for the sake of five righteous men, could they have been found there.

How precious, how beautiful in the sight of God must a soul be that is decked with the charms of grace! To guard and guide souls whose innocence pleases God, to multiply the number of the children of God, — such is the sublime end of the great work of *Christian education.* In Catholic institutions there is always to be found a chosen number of young people who have never stained the robe of their baptism, who preserve unsullied the innocence of their souls, or who have regained it if lost, and who guard it under the divine protection of the sacraments. Doubtless the eye of man does not always distinguish these souls with certainty. Like the young man in the gospel, who had kept all the commandments, and whom the good Master regarded with love, they are unnoticed by the crowd. But God knows them, God loves them, and the sight of them arrests His avenging arm, already raised to strike the guilty.

Let us imagine a group of young men, penetrated and animated by these lofty considerations, who resolve firmly to keep their souls pure from sin, and who employ prayer, the sacraments, the influence of word and example, and especially the service and imitation of Mary, as the means to this end. Will they not be the most precious jewel in that crown of honor which encircles the brow of the Immaculate Virgin?

The foundation of such a sodality had become an absorbing idea with the venerable Father Rem. In his view, perfect devotion to Mary should consist in serving her by an immaculate purity. He desired to form a gathering of true children of Mary, among whom there should not be a single soul stained with sin.

Only those were received who had been previously consecrated to Mary in some other sodality of the college. On their entrance, after a month's probation, they bound themselves to a life which should be not only edifying in the sight of their companions, but of the strictest interior purity and sanctity. Weekly confession, frequent communion, pious conversations and meditation furnished them abundant helps to perseverance in their sublime purpose.

Their rule excluded from all privileges and indulgences any who might be living in a state of mortal sin. By the very fact that a member had lost sanctifying grace, he ceased to share in the spiritual favors of the sodality until the moment of his return to God.

We may not lightly tax this design of the venerable father with indiscretion, or regard it as the result of a pious but unpractical simplicity, for it received the highest possible approval. The Sovereign Pontiff, Paul V., by his brief of Jan. 5, 1615, indorsed this pious association and granted it special indulgences.[1] It is true that it encountered much adverse criticism, but it maintained its position, and produced fruits of eminent holiness.[2]

In several colleges the most devout members of the sodalities, thus united themselves in the profession of a more fervent piety, and a closer imitation of the virtues of Mary. They ordinarily placed themselves under the protection of Mary Immaculate, thus rendering homage to the spotless purity of their Mother, and supplying an additional safeguard to their own chastity. Is not this beautiful virtue the most precious treasure of the young and the earnest of all other virtues? They bear this treasure in a fragile casket, but if they would preserve it intact, is it not under the

---

[1] *Der ehrwürdige P. Jacob Rem*, already quoted, Book I. chap. II. § 4.

[2] KROPF, *Hist. prov. S. J. Germaniæ superioris*, pp. 94 et 195.

protection of the Blessed Virgin that they should place it? How touching was that inspiration of a father in the college at Namur, who, about the year 1670, invited select members of different sodalities to form a special association to obtain from God the gift of angelic purity!

They fortified themselves every week with the bread of angels, and celebrated with great devotion the feasts of the Blessed Sacrament and of the Mother of God;[1] so as to have constantly before their eyes the mirror of justice and holiness on which they wished to form their souls, they recited every day the little office of the Immaculate Conception. Who can tell us with what joy the Queen of Heaven and the celestial court looked on so many thousands of children and young men, who at the reunions of fervor, as they were called, kept their souls pure for eternal life, and, far from defiling them with the contact of earthly things, ornamented them with all the virtues and beauty of grace.

[1] The rules approved of by the Bishop of Cambray were printed in 1680, at Namur. See DE BACKER, *Bibliographie:* Namur.

CHAPTER V

The Sodalities outside the Colleges

TO serve God under the protection of the Blessed Virgin Mary, keep our faith and piety in the world, of which Our Saviour Jesus Christ condemned the spirit and bad works, fulfil the duties of our state in life in fortifying ourselves with the example and encouragements that we meet in a reunion of sincere Christians, give ourselves up to some works of charity corresponding with our means,—this is, in a few words, the end proposed by the different sodalities in the world.

Piety is useful and obliging, said Saint Paul; it is not then to be wondered at to see numerous works of charity and mercy originating from the pious assemblies of which we are sketching the history. There would be no end if we did not purposely limit ourselves to citing only a few of the examples of the different kinds of apostleship that they undertook.

Let us first speak of those in Rome; nowhere will we better find the spirit which animated them, and the broadness of views which their directors took.

In 1593 a sodality of noblemen was formed under the direction of the venerable F. Marcello Mastrilli, who was martyred forty years afterwards in Japan. A century after, it could pride itself on having more than ninety of its members elevated to the dignity of the cardinalate, and among these princes of the church, six who occupied the chair of Saint Peter: Urban VIII., Alexander VII., Clement IX., Clement X., Innocent XI., and Innocent XII. Its principal work was to settle disputes: among the impetuous spirits of the south, quarrels and deadly feuds were not rare; so the associates of the Sodality of the Assumption exerted themselves to honor the Queen of Peace by reconciling enemies. To accomplish this object they divided amongst themselves the sixteen quarters of Rome, and their truly Christian influence produced such good results, that the parish priests contented themselves, as soon as a difficulty arose, with reporting the case to them to restore peace in the family.[1] The sodality kept a register in which were inscribed the pardons granted in the name of Mary.

The following year two were formed for the

---

[1] H. S. part V., Book XVI., no. 32. Litt. Ann. 1593, Dom. Prof.

working people; one for the masters, and one for the journeymen, in a short time the latter increased to two hundred. To the regular approaching of the Holy Table, to the pious pilgrimages made together, and to the weekly works of penance, were added visits to the hospitals. They divided amongst themselves the numerous hospitals of Rome, and on Sunday they took pleasure in bringing to the sick, together with the consolations of charity, modest gifts, fruit and dainties, which were always received with delight. These zealous works were rewarded with special graces; some distinguished themselves in the service of their masters, by their correct morals and by their example of industry, some were drawn to a more perfect life; in one year, ten of these young men embraced the poor and austere life of the Capuchins.[1] F. Aquaviva, to stimulate the zeal of the young F. Simon Franco, their director, yielded to him a part of the Roman College.[2] The sodality of the Nativity devoted itself to consoling and ameliorating the lot of prisoners. The cardinals and the Pope encouraged this work of mercy, and sent to the children of Mary help to encourage their generosity. Every month they procured for the prisoners a great feast, on the day on which the

---

[1] Litt. Ann. 1594, Dom. Prof., H. S. part V., book XVI., 33.
[2] Op. Patrignani, I. 241.

general communion united them. This was the character of the sodalities at Rome, and it did not differ in other parts. Let us content ourselves with citing the work of a few of the branches in Spain, Italy, and the northern countries.

At Cordova, the sodalities interested themselves in the poor prisoners, who were easily exposed to be unjustly punished for the want of means to plead their cases. Two members, one a priest, one a lawyer, went every week to the prisons to look after cases still undecided;[1] others gathered together, on certain days, from four to five hundred beggars and vagabonds, and brought them to the church of the Society, to prepare them for confession.[2] Seville, a considerable commercial port in the past, saw established in 1608, a sodality composed entirely of lawyers, who undertook to plead their cases for the poor and for strangers, and despatched them without cost. They settled many a dispute, thus avoiding legal entanglements which would often last very long.[3] Sodalities of the same kind were founded at Milan, Naples,[4] and other places. Those of Naples were the most celebrated and the most varied. Father Spinelli[5] in 1613, counted fifteen. The

[1] H. S., Part V., Book XVI., 34.   [2] Litt. Ann. 1592, 1609.
[3] Litt. Ann. 1592, 1609.   [4] H. S, 1617, 7.
[5] Maria Deipara, thronus Dei, chap. 40.

confraternity of the Purification devoted itself to the reform of the galley-slaves and the conversion of the Moors, Turks, and Ethiopians, and brought them together by hundreds to instruct them and prepare them for baptism and liberty. In the space of seven years, three hundred of these wretches renounced their deeply-rooted superstitions. Cardinal Bellarmine and Pope Paul V. took a great interest in this work of devotion. The associates of the sodality of the Nativity, mostly fathers of families, contributed large sums secretly to save from shame and misery families fallen by reverses in business. Schoolmasters — Naples counted three hundred — united under the protection of Mary to learn to devote themselves to the ungrateful work of education : this proved the beginning of a marvellous renovation of piety among the young. The author also mentions the sodalities of the sailors and fishermen of the suburb of Chiaia, of merchants, workingmen, and especially of clerics, of whom we shall speak afterwards. Four years later he could have added the sodality of Our Lady of Mount Carmel, a strange and admirable institution, which made, of a receptacle of vice, a home of virtue, and changed a prison, a den of guilt, into an edifying retreat. The sweet Virgin Mary, who never abandoned sinners, and whose goodness ought never to suffer any one to despair, loved to form a court of devoted servants in the midst of those justly condemned by human laws. It is of these that a pious writer truthfully said: "You ask me what miracles the sodality has performed? I give you my word that it resuscitates the dead: men who had passed years in sin, victims of stinging remorse, have found, in the sodality of the Immaculate Virgin, the grace of God, pure lives, and the peace of a good conscience." [1]

The sodalities of France were no less varied nor less active. Father Crasset, who for a long time governed the Professed House of Paris, tells us that at the meetings, which took place every fortnight, a delegation of four or five members was formed to distribute alms at Notre Dame, at the Hotel-Dieu, to the modest poor, and to the prisoners.[2] At the novitiate in the Faubourg Saint Germain there met an assembly, who prided themselves that amongst their members were the princes Ferdinand and Charles of Lorraine, and several other distinguished personages. But besides these two sodalities reserved for the rich, there were two others for their servants, "so that, when accompanying their

[1] Le Chef d'Œuvre de Dieu, by Binet, S. J., 3d part, chap. XVI.

[2] Des Congrégations de Notre Dame, Paris, 1693, reedited by Father Carayon in 1863, page 158.

masters, instead of idly waiting for them during the two hours that the meetings lasted, they also had the occasion to perform the same devotions in honor of the Blessed Virgin Mary."[1] It was thus that the zeal of the directors made them all to all, according to the expression of St. Paul, to gain all to Jesus Christ and to His Holy Mother.

But we would expose our readers to the annoyance of monotony, if we were to enumerate the annals of the host of sodalities spread over Europe, Asia, and America, by simply relating or mentioning their works. Let us content ourselves with stating two advantages which they obtained, and of which the importance was considerable.

We may say that the frequentation of the sacraments is the measure of fervor and piety in the church; for they are the nourishment of the soul. Outside of this divine source of grace, there is no Christian life; on the contrary, this life is strengthened and becomes fruitful, as often as it is thus refreshed. Now, for one who remembers the condition of the church in the sixteenth century, and the weakening of the faith that heresy had more or less caused in every country, it is easy to conclude that, outside the Easter com-

---

[1] Des Congrégations de Notre Dame, Paris, 1693, re-edited by Father Carayon in 1863, page 83.

munion, the use of the sacraments had fallen into decay.

The rules of the sodalities which recommended monthly communions, contributed wonderfully to re-establishing Christian fervor in this respect, and from the sodalities this pious practice became the custom of the faithful. In fact, in 1616,[1] by the efforts of the sodality of the Assumption, the solemnity of general communion was begun in Rome: each month it was transferred to a different church; the people were prepared by sermons on the reception of the great Sacrament, as they had been attracted by the decoration of the church in which extraordinary splendor was displayed. A special sodality was founded to take charge of the preparations for this monthly feast. The plenary indulgence which the Sovereign Pontiff granted was a powerful means to encourage the work, and little by little the sodalities introduced the custom in other cities.

In Belgium, as attested by the annals of different colleges, it was the beginning of a constant increase in the number of communions. In the church of the Professed House of Anvers this feast of Holy Communion on the first Sunday of the month attracted such numbers that the eucharistic bread was given to eight thousand of

[1] H. S. parte V., lib. XVII., 45.

the faithful;[1] in the church of Saint Francis
Xavier, at Bruges, from sixty thousand in 1639,
the annual number of communions rose to one
hundred thousand in 1650, and to two hundred
thousand in 1675.[2]

The pious custom of the forty hours' adoration
was instituted in 1556, by Father Mortagne, at
Macerata, in Italy,[3] and at the same time it would
appear that Father Joseph, a capuchin of Milan,
introduced it in the latter city:[4] it was propagated
by the zeal of the sodalities, and spread all over
the Catholic world. It was but natural that the
servants of Mary should unite their efforts to expiate the licentious rout of the carnival, and fight
against sacrilegious profanations with arms of
prayer.[5] In 1599, the city of Louvain saw Justus
Lipsius, then Prefect of the sodality, take up this
practice, and, giving the example to his brethren,
remain for hours in adoration before the Blessed
Sacrament. The associates, after having, at the
beginning of Lent, joined in this act of reparation,
met again, towards the end of the season of pen-

---

[1] Annales Antwerpienses, du P. Papebroch, IV. p. 352.

[2] Notice Historique sur l'Ancien Collège des Jésuites à Bruges, dans les Annales de la Société de l'Emulation de la Flandre, 1884.

[3] H. S. Part I. book XIV. 10.

[4] Chardon, Histoire des Sacrements, l'Eucharistie, chap. 13.

[5] Hist. MSE. Coll. Lovan., Archives du Royaume de Belgique, No. 772.

ance, to honor the passion of Our Lord during the night of Holy Thursday.

It was at Rome, however, that the forty hours' devotion was celebrated, since 1593, with particular pomp, the expression of the peculiar piety that animated the Sodality of the Assumption. Frederick Cœsio, Duke of Aqua-Sparta, who was the Prefect, wished to give the people a public manifestation which, until then had been only of a private character. He obtained the permission of the Sovereign Pontiff, Clement VIII., to transfer it to the church of the Professed House. This beautiful temple adorned for the occasion, at the expense of the associates, was visited, during the three days of the carnival, by all the pious confraternities of the city; the Pope himself celebrated Mass there, and granted special indulgences to all the faithful who joined in the adoration and the communion of reparation.

If we add to the general communion every month, and to the forty hours' devotion, the solemnity with which the associates celebrated the day of their patron saint, and the principal feasts of the Blessed Virgin Mary, we can have an idea of the good the sodality has done in the Catholic world. Have not the children of Mary reason to be happy and proud, in thinking of so many works of zeal and of piety established by their predecessors?

It is also a very laudable custom which was introduced into many sodalities, every year to consecrate several days to meditation on the great truths which are the foundation and the support of Christian life. In the midst of the world, where one goes astray seeking temporal happiness, and so easily loses sight of the only road to true and lasting happiness and eternal salvation, there is danger of fervent Christians falling away. The sodalities offered, it is true, powerful means against the seductions of the world in the regular meetings; one can see, however, that it was necessary to offer to the clients of Mary an opportunity to refresh their fervor by a course of special exercises undergone in retreat. In this retreat, which was generally made before the feast of their patron saint, to prepare them for the renewal of their act of consecration, the associates applied themselves, according to the expression of Scripture, "to scrutinizing their ways;" remembering that there are broad and flowery paths before them, but that they are too far from the narrow path which the Saviour recommends, and they applied themselves to entering courageously into the one which opens to us the liberty of the children of God. They met twice, and even three times a day, to listen, not to eloquent sermons, but to practical and useful instructions, to meditate themselves on the subjects proposed, so as to make personal resolutions. Can it not easily be believed that these retreats of men, by the grace of God, and the protection of Mary, should have borne marvellous fruits and formed good Christians? They gave to more than one country those valiant generations of Catholics really worthy of the glorious name, of which Cardinal de Bausset wrote [1] at the beginning of this century: "It is still remembered in the principal commercial cities, that never were there more order and tranquillity, more honesty in business transactions, fewer failures, and less depravity, than when the sodalities existed; the Jesuits had the talent of interesting in them all the professions, and all the social institutions; they endeavored to keep in all the states the regularity of morals, the spirit of subordination, the wise economy, which preserved peace and harmony in the families, and assured the prosperity of empires."

[1] Life of Fénelon, Book L

CHAPTER VI

Sodalities of Priests

AS the Blessed Virgin is the mother of all the virtues, Christian piety also recognizes in her the mother of the virtues proper to the priesthood. The Queen of the Apostles and Doctors, she is also the model of the great sanctity which God demands of his priests; she is the mother and foster-mother of the apostolic zeal which ought to animate their hearts. How natural it was that the sodalities should welcome in their midst those whose high vocation made the devotion to Mary more specially necessary to them.

We have said before that priests in large numbers, and even religious, inscribed their names in the sodalities of Cologne, Saint Omer, and Anvers. The Latin sodality of the latter city was usually honored with the presence of the canons of the cathedral;[1] at Bruges the sodality of the élite counted a great number of ecclesiastics;

---

[1] Précis Historiques, 1882, April-June. Les anciens Congrégations de la ville d'Anvers.

several bishops inscribed their names on its register or accepted the title of prefect.[1] It was the same in other places. Those who in the fervent reunions of the college had shown their love to the Blessed Virgin, at the same time that they had developed the germ of their vocation, did not renounce the glorious adoption with which they were honored; and tried, when possible, to frequent some sodality of the city where they exercised their holy ministry.

In the cities where the clergy were numerous, it was even possible to establish sodalities exclusively for ecclesiastics.

At Louvain the students of theology who, until then, had been united to those of law, constituted themselves into a separate sodality in 1608, under the title of the Immaculate Conception. There were generally more than a hundred on the rolls, and for thirty years they had as their director the zealous and learned Becanus, professor of Holy Scripture at the theological college of the society. By the ardor of their devotion to the Blessed Virgin, and by the practice of pious reading, procured for them from a special library, they prepared themselves to become one day ministers of the gospel as pious as they were learned.[2] In

[1] Notice sur l'ancien Collège des Jesuites à Bruges.
[2] Hist. Soc. Jesu. Lovan, MS., Archives du Royaume, No. 772.

1611, twelve canons and some other priests of Cologne inaugurated a new sodality, which soon numbered forty members, and increased the zeal of the priests in defending the Catholic faith.[1] It continued during all the seventeenth century.

In the same year, at the college of Naples, under the title of the Assumption, was founded the sodality of clergymen, about the organization of which Father Spinelli has left us useful information. Two years after its foundation, it counted four hundred members ; the flower of the secular clergy and fourteen bishops inscribed their names and assisted at the meetings as often as their duties allowed them.

Father Pavone, who had undertaken this work, directed it until 1637, and had the consolation of seeing it extend to different cities of the kingdom. It was continued by his brethren. It is known that Saint Vincent de Paul introduced a similar work in France in the same year, 1637.

The object of the clerical sodalities of Naples was twofold. First, to form devoted and industrious pastors, for which purpose the younger members met once a week in the afternoon, to instruct one another in the art of preaching, teaching catechism, and advancing the faithful in the service of God. The object of the Sunday meet-

[1] Reiffenberg, Historia, S. J., ad Rhenum Inferiorem, No. 467.

ings was higher. The more select among the very devout, who, after a few days of spiritual exercises, offered themselves in a special manner to Mary, and who, under the name of Oblates, sought to promote the glory of God, met again on Sunday evenings to give themselves up to practices of humility and mortification, to examine their consciences, and perform other works of piety. Every six months they renewed their offering of themselves to the Blessed Virgin, after having prepared themselves for this act by a few days of retreat and a general confession.

The fruits of sanctity which this pious confraternity produced in the city and diocese of Naples, were such as everyone can readily suppose; it is useless to speak of them at length.[1] Is not the piety of the Catholic people influenced by the priest who governs them? "As is the priest, so are the people," is a maxim consecrated by experience and by the history of the Church. In the ordinary course of things, bishops and priests sincerely devoted to the Virgin of Virgins, and, united by a community of views, necessarily succeed in forming their flock to the practice of Christian virtues.

The sodalities of priests founded in Spain deserve our special attention; they justly claimed the honor of having worked ardently to maintain

[1] Spinelli; op. cit. page 570, chap. 40, No. 16.

and propagate the Catholic belief of the most glorious of Mary's privileges, her Immaculate Conception. It is not within our scope to enter into the causes which seemed at one time to menace that belief so dear to us.[1] The Sorbonne in France, the University of Louvain, the King of Spain, by a decree of 1456, had solemnly affirmed it; the fathers of the council of Trent admitted it almost unanimously, and the Order of Saint Francis professed and defended it with an unflinching constancy. The Society of Jesus, according to a revelation made to the lay-brother, Blessed Alphonsus Rodriguez, had received the mission to protect against her detractors this greatest glory of Mary;[2] its zeal for the accomplishment of this work communicated itself to the sodalities. In every country it founded one under the title of the Immaculate Conception, and we can easily believe that the celebration of this special feast, made with the accustomed solemnity, was not without reviving and maintaining everywhere belief in this privilege of the Virgin. That of Lima, in Peru, composed of a hundred priests, presided over by the archbishop, prolonged the feast of the Immaculate Conception for an en-

---

[1] Malou, l'Immaculée Conception de la Bienheureuse Vierge Marie, vol. II. chap. XIII.

[2] Natalis, De cœlesti conversatione, part 2, chap. 7, § 1.

tire week.[1] Towards 1616, the whole of Spain exerted itself, and began to oppose with an irresistible ardor the current which was carrying away some bold minds from the common belief. At the Professed House of Seville, there was a sodality of priests under the invocation of the Immaculate Conception. The canon Vasquez de Leca, one of its most fervent members,[2] thought that the best way to stop the controversy among the theologians would be to have recourse to the authority of the chief pastors. He therefore collected letters from the bishops testifying the faith of their flock, and presented himself at the court of Philip III., to beseech him in their name to take in hand the defence of the Catholic faith. During these negotiations the sodality of Astige joined that of Seville, and made a vow to defend the glorious prerogative unto death. An embassy was sent to Rome, which obtained a decree prohibiting the public denial of the Immaculate Conception. The universities of Alcala and Evora, and all the academies of learning in Spain and Portugal, did not cease, after that first step, to excite against their adversaries the common feeling of the faithful towards the privilege of Mary; it was certainly not from a lack of ardor on their part that the

[1] Nadasi, Annales Mariani, 347, H. S. 1619, 183.
[2] H. S. 1616, 130.

Holy See did not then define as a dogma a truth which was believed by the Catholic world. One day, at Seville, a preacher dared to utter a doubt on the common belief. Father John Pineda had hardly heard it when he called the people around his pulpit, and, in an earnest extempore discourse, glorified Our Lady with so much eloquence that applause broke out on every side, and eighty thousand crowns were immediately collected to raise to the glory of Mary a trophy, on which was inscribed: "The Blessed Virgin was conceived without sin."[1] Spanish piety understood that one cannot refuse to the Mother of God any glory at all compatible with the nature of a creature. "*De qua natus est Jesus*, of whom was born Jesus." "Meditate on this simple clause," said Saint Thomas de Villanova, "and you will understand what favors you must attribute to it."

We might appropriately add to this chapter another institution, to which a sodality of the college Louis-le-Grand gave birth; we will follow the narrative of M. Laquet, a member of the Congregation of Foreign Missions.[2]

Encouraged by the advice of Father Bagot, their director, several students, already members

---

[1] Nadasi, No. 850, ad ann. 1637.

[2] Lettres à l'évêque de Langres sur la Congrégation des Missions Étrangères: Paris, Gaume, 1842.

of the sodality, about the year 1650, formed a more particular society, whose object was to give itself up to works of zeal and charity among the poor of the city, as well as among their fellow disciples of the college. As the love of God, and absolute self-denial of all which is not self, were the only link which united them, all that they possessed was in common. They established themselves in the Rue St. Dominique. This was their status when Father Rhodes, the great missionary of Tonquin, arrived from Rome, and presented himself at the college of Clermont. Providence seems to have guided him, and to have put him in communication with the director of the first apostles called to the great work of the foreign missions. Father Bagot introduced to him his young associates, and spoke to him of the zeal with which they entered into all that could procure the glory of God and the good of their neighbor. Animated as they were with these sublime views, they, on their part, beheld with as much admiration as emotion, a religious who had renounced his country, crossed the seas, and courted martyrdom for the salvation of souls. Anxious to hear from the mouth of the apostle himself an account of his works and of his sufferings, they begged Father Bagot to procure for them the happiness of a second visit from the missionary. Father

Rhodes gratified their wish. The enthusiasm, and the desire for martyrdom which inflamed their hearts, and the resolution they took to leave all for the gospel, appeared to him to be inspired by grace. He could not help saying, as he left, "I have just found in these young men better dispositions than those I have sought in the seminaries."

It may be said, adds the author whose narrative we are transcribing, that it is the impression, so vivid, and at the same time so deep, made at these interviews, which nourished and fortified in the souls of these young associates, gave rise to the establishment of the Seminary of Foreign Missions. It is in these pious assemblies, and under the protection of their peerless Patroness, that they received the grace which was given them, to go and preach Jesus Christ to the heathen. They were like a little branch, from which has sprung a tree great in the number of Bishops and Vicars Apostolic, that have been chosen from among them, for the East and for the West.

CHAPTER VII

Examples of Holiness in the Sodalities

THE practice of spiritual and corporal works of mercy, as also of all the Christian virtues, highly recommended our pious confraternities. We cannot, however, even entertain the thought of relating all the edifying examples contained in our annals. They would find a better place in a separate historical notice, if they were known as the acts of persons whose real names are on record. The anonymous, unfortunately, takes away a great deal of their interest, but it will not be amiss to bring to mind the memory of some well-known sodalists, who, rising to eminent sanctity, have merited to be employed in great works of God for the salvation of souls, or who have deserved the consideration of the Church to such a degree, that she has proposed them for our imitation in authorizing their public veneration. In the first part of this history we have mentioned several saints, or those beatified, who have propagated or favored the sodalities.

After Fathers Leonius, Costerus, and Rem, after the venerable Edmund Campian, Bl. Peter Canisius and St. Charles Borromeo, let us first record the angelic John Berchmans, the paragon of students. The authors of his life[1] show him to us, at the College of Malines, so zealous for the honor of Mary that his example and his words drew several of his schoolmates to be admitted among the number of the privileged children of the Blessed Virgin, while he himself, to be more agreeable to his Mother, worked with a holy solicitude to perfect himself. This excellent young man applied himself seriously to his education. At the beginning of every month, he went to the director of the sodality to learn from him what fault he had most to correct, what penance to impose, and what pious exercise to perform in honor of Mary and his patron for the month. Everyone knows with what devotion he made the pilgrimage to Notre Dame de Montaigue, which had then begun to be celebrated for its miracles. It was not, it was said, the least of her miracles to have caused such an angel to appear in mortal flesh. Every day he renewed his act of consecration to Mary. It was to her intercession that he attributed all the graces that the Lord had granted him, and in particular the precious boon of his

---

[1] "The Rev. Father J. Eudes," by A. Ledoré: Paris, 1869, page 154.

religious state. But as he also felt a sacred jealousy for her honor, he signed with his blood the promise to defend unto death the prerogative of her Immaculate Conception. After this angel of purity, whom heaven envied the earth, and whom the Queen of Angels called to her celestial court when still very young, another son of Mary must be mentioned, who, about the same period, after having acquired the noblest virtues in the sodality, was chosen by Providence to found a school of apostleship. John Eudes, as the author of his life relates, in 1615 entered the Jesuit college at Caen, and it was not long before he was admitted to the sodality of the students, whom he served as a model. It was especially in this saintly company, so well calculated to preserve the innocence of young men, that he conceived his tender attachment and devotion to the Mother of God. At the age of fourteen he made a perpetual vow of chastity, and, after having united himself forever to the Most Pure of Virgins, he omitted nothing that could testify to her his devotion. Nay, he did not pass a single day without showing her some proof of his piety, following, in this, the example of the holy apostle whose name he bore, and to whom Jesus, in dying, recommended his beloved Mother; so entirely did he live only for her honor, and that of her Son.

"I know a servant of God"—he wrote later in speaking of himself—"who had received from His Divine bounty a number of graces through the intercession of the Blessed Virgin; one cause of his happiness was, that he had been a student at the Jesuit College, and had been admitted into the sodality of the Blessed Virgin, where Our Saviour showed him great mercy by means of his Holy Mother." The long career of the venerable John Eudes was worthy of this auspicious education; he bequeathed to the *Eudistes*, whom he had founded in 1643, the spirit of apostolic zeal and the devotion to Mary which had rendered his works so fruitful.

He was not the only founder of an order whose glory was reflected on the sodality; Saint Francis de Sales, Prefect of that established at the college of Clermont, the Blessed Peter Fourrier, founder of the Canons of Our Saviour, M. Olier, founder of Saint Sulpice, M. de Montfort, founder of the missionaries of the Holy Ghost, and others· gloried in having imbibed in the sodalities their tender love for Mary.

At the college of Fribourg, towards the end of the sixteenth century, there lived a young student who by his literary success was the pride of his classes. A fervent and exemplary member of the sodality, still flourishing, as in the time of the Blessed Canisius, the young man practised in this school of piety all the strong solid virtues, which alone can guarantee, later on in life, the best-tempered characters against the shock of the world. Arrived at the age when it was time to decide on his profession, he prayed fervently to God, and decided to study law. The spirit of mortification and self-denial seemed sufficient to preserve him from the attacks of evil. As his modesty had procured him the esteem of everyone, several noblemen of Suabia asked him to be their guide in a journey they undertook to the principal cities of France, Spain, Germany, and Italy. Having begun it under Heaven's protection, the tour was successfully accomplished; on their return to their homes, after six years' absence, the companions of the saintly member of the sodality paid homage to his virtues and to the zeal he had shown for their instruction as well as for their pleasure. Advanced to the Doctorate of Laws, he became the attorney of the poor, and the invincible defender of justice. It was this virtue so often exposed to violation even among Christians, that merited him a grace which was to be the source of many more. Irritated by an injustice aimed at his honor, he renounced the dangers of the legal profession to follow a more noble career, the voluntary and apostolic poverty of the Capuchins — the world praised Fidelis of Sigmaringen, who had become the advocate of the cause of heaven, and the minister of God, and remained so until the day when a glorious martyrdom crowned his humble but powerful ministry. The Church has graced him with the honors of her altars.

The Sodality of the Roman College boasts of counting amongst its members two more illustrious clients of Mary. The Blessed Leonard of Porto-Maurizio, who towards 1689 followed the course of this celebrated college, was the model of its sodalities. The authors of his life tell us that the young Leonard attended all the pious exercises of the meetings with great edification; he went with fervor to celebrate the feasts which were observed by the different sodalities, and in particular loved to visit the oratory of Father Gravitá, commonly known by the soubriquet of Caravitá. It will be remembered that in this oratory, erected under the protection of the Blessed Virgin,[1] the most fervent of the brethren assembled on Fridays to honor the Passion of Our Lord by prayer and corporal penances; strange as it may seem to our delicate natures, this practice still exists in defiance of the spirit of the word, like an eloquent protestation in

[1] H. S. 1616, n. 14; 1623, n. 5.

favor of the folly of penitence and of the cross. Is it not here, perhaps, that the Blessed Leonard began his tender devotion to Jesus suffering? He was the most zealous propagator of the holy exercise of the Way of the Cross; his love for Mary, Mother of Sorrows, was equally great.

John de Rossi, whom the reigning Sovereign Pontiff has latterly raised on our altars, was, during his course at the Roman College, a member of the sodality of the Scaletta. The Director, who esteemed his great virtues, made use of him to effect much good among the scholars; but it was especially during the vacation that the Blessed John availed himself of his influence to turn them from evil and the fatal results of idleness. He joined with them in innocent games, and agreeable amusements, and taught them to take pleasure in relieving the sick, helping the poor, and encouraging the working-men in their hard day's labor. This noble love of devotion to the service of the unfortunate, animated his whole career. Having become a priest in 1721, he consecrated to them his fortune and his life, and it is by this exercise of sacerdotal charity that he reached his high degree of sanctity.[1]

We might further mention other saints who have frequented or directed the confraternities of

---

[1] Butler, Lives of the Saints, May 23.

the Virgin Mother; we might give the names of youths whose pure and innocent lives have been bequeathed to the remembrance of their brethren of the sodality, in biographical notices,[1] although there was not then the same eagerness as now to proclaim the virtues of the deceased. We will limit ourselves to a few names, justly honored in the history of the Church, who reflect credit on the work of the sodalities.

Cardinal Frederick Borromeo, the worthy successor to the name and archbishopric of his holy uncle, Charles, succeeded him also in his attachment for the servants of Mary. He had for a long time been the example of the sodalists of Bologna. Penetrated with the sentiments of piety which he had imbibed in the confraternity, he wished to establish several in his diocese; he formed one of young people whom he called "Children of Our Lady," and caused to wear a medal with this inscription: *Monstra te esse matrem;* and another one of older men, who, having more authority, promised to honor the mother of God by reprimanding all those whom they heard using immodest words. The fruits of these were visible in the cities where they were established. He

[1] Le Parfait Écolier, ou Vie de Plurieurs Étudiants, Amiens, Carron, 1805: De vita Arnaldi Boreti, Senatoris Tolesani, Possino, Paris, 1639.

established a third one, of which he was the head and director, and which he called his secret fraternity, the first rule of which was to protest openly and manfully when they found themselves among persons licentious enough to mock or speak against the devotion of the Blessed Virgin.[1] This holy prelate on his deathbed forbade that any mausoleum should be erected to him; but he ordered that he should be buried at the foot of Our Lady, and that this simple inscription in Latin should be put on his tomb:—

> FREDERICUS, CARDINALIS BORROMÆUS
> ARCHIEPISCOPUS MEDIOLANENSIS
> SUB PRÆSIDIO B. MARIÆ VIRGINIS
> HIC QUIESCIT IN PACE.

Vincent Carafa, of the ducal family of Andria, after having been in his youth a sodalist of the Annunciation at Rome, later on directed the celebrated sodality of the Nativity at Naples. The author of his life[2] has given us, in his naïve and quaint style, most edifying details of the zeal of the holy director.

"Father Vincent was at first surprised at the

---

[1] Crasset, Des Congrégations de Notre Dame, édition Carayon, page 165.

[2] The life of R. F. Carafa, 7th General of the Society of Jesus. ... Done into French by Th. LeBlanc, S. J., Liége, MDCLIII., page 76, 389.

pitiable state of this sodality, which was before so flourishing in number and in the practice of virtues, whereas now it was so dwarfed and diminished that it could hardly be called a body, and its devout exercises were almost discontinued . . . which often happens in communities where there are few people: because, as live coals, if there are many together, kindle one another and each one burns in the fire of all, and when there are a few, they go out little by little, so men incite one another when in great numbers, and grow cold, and chill one another when in small numbers. . . . But it pleased God to help the enterprise, and after having put the mind of the father at ease, to draw thence great profit for souls and for his glory. . . . Having placed his hope in the Lord and in the Blessed Virgin, he accepted the charge, and said to himself, 'In future one must think only of God and the sodality.' He persuaded himself to work for these gentlemen in such a way as to make them all saints. So every time that the Father who had been given him as a companion in this office, came into his room to speak to him on any topic, he received him with these words, which came from his heart: 'What news from the sodality? Are those gentlemen becoming saints?' Not only the number but their fervor increased, and, what is more remarkable, he employed no artifice in seeking or inviting them: the renown alone of Father Vincent, and the desire to have a saint as a master and spiritual father, attracted the crowds, and this was the secret of his success.

"Having thus reconstructed the confraternity in the point of numbers, it was not long before he could restore it to the original works of charity, principally the weekly visit on Tuesdays to the hospital for incurables. . . . Father Vincent was always the first and served as an example to all in the practice of virtue. . . .

"Having firmly re-established the first observances, he began to add others; and the work confined to his care answered the expectations of his zeal." He often thought of the account he would have to render to God of these young men, "each of whom would have made a family holy, and all together a city, if they could have had a director who could have made them saints." Father Carafa was elected General of the Society of Jesus in 1647.

Might we not here mention the celebrated missionary of Naples, Saint Francis de Geronimo, and of the modest but holy sodality of mechanics which he directed toward the end of the seventeenth century? "You are the chosen flock which Providence has confided to my care," he said to them, "henceforth I am yours." Those were not useless words. When, at the meetings on Sunday morning, these good working-men saw the Saint in the presence of the Victim on our altars, when they heard him make the usual exhortation, they felt penetrated with the same ardor. He interested them in his missions; he made use of them for the salvation of souls; he made them zealots, and they were called "the Brothers of the Missions." It was like a holy legion always at war with the devil, going everywhere by order of their admirable director, calling the negligent to the instructions, gathering hearers around the cross in some public place, preaching by example, penance, and humility, and deriving from their zeal the beginning of their own progress. But we must conclude, and refer our readers to the history of the celebrated apostle of Naples.[1]

After this roll of saints, of whom some have been formally recognized as such by the Church, would it be rashness to mention an emperor whom a contemporary, without any intention of flattering, called the new Constantine, greater by his virtues than by his high position? Without wishing to put him on the same level, let us recall this illustrious servant of Mary whom the sodality of

[1]. History of S. Francis de Geronimo, by Father Julien Bach, Metz, 1867.

Louvain gloried in having inscribed on its register, and who counted among his titles of honor that of being a member of the sodality.

When Ferdinand II. was still only King of Hungary and Bohemia, he made this entry with his own hand in the book of that sodality: "Anno Domini 1618, die septima novembris, Ferdinandus, Ungariæ Bohemiæque Rex, archidux Austriæ, Sodalis Beatissimæ Dei Genitricis Virginis Mariæ, scripsit, sub cujus præsidio se semper commendat."

On becoming emperor, he desired to sign a second time, in this his new position, that he was a member of the sodality of the Virgin Mother, in order to show the world that he esteemed this title as highly, as any that accrued to him from the most splendid crowns of the universe. His son, in his turn, also enlisted under the standard of Mary, and his successor, Ferdinand III., signed this beautiful pledge of devotion, which has often been reproduced, and which claims mention here in honor of the Blessed Virgin: —

ILLIUS EGO CŒTUS SUB INVOCATIONE TUA CONGREGATI,
AUGUSTISSIMA MARIA,
ME LIBENS ET MERITO UNUM PROFITEOR:
TIBI EGO ME MEOSQUE, CONJUGEM AC LIBEROS,
TIBI ROMANUM IMPERIUM, CUI DEUS ME PRÆFECIT,
TIBI REGNA A MAJORIBUS ACCEPTA,
TIBI TUTELÆQUE TUÆ POPULUM ET EXERCITUS MEOS,
TIBI TUOQUE FILIO MILITANTES,
COMMITTO.

TU ME IN TUUM ADMITTE,
QUI FILIO TUO, QUI TIBI, QUI UTRIUSQUE HONORI
VIVO, REGNO, PUGNO,
TUUS IGITUR EGO ERO,
MARIA,
TUI ERUNT QUICUMQUE MEI,
TUA ERUNT DITIONES ET REGNA MEA ET IMPERIUM,
TUI POPULI ET EXERCITUS.
TU EOS PROTEGE, TU EIS VINCE,
TU IN EIS REGNA ET IMPERA,
ITA VOVEO,
MDCXL.
TUUS PIETATE ET JUSTITIA,
FERDINANDUS.

"With joy and with justice, I profess myself a member of the sodality formed under Thy invocation, Most August Mary. To Thee I commit myself and mine, my spouse and my children: to Thee I confide the Roman empire, over which God has set me, and the kingdoms which I hold from my ancestors: to Thee do I commend my people and my armies, who combat for Thee and Thy Son. Receive me, then, as Thine own, who live and reign and battle for Thy Son, for Thee, and for the honor of you both. Thine, therefore, shall I be, O Mary! Thine shall be all that are mine: Thine my domains, my kingdoms, my empire: Thine my subjects in peace and in war. Do Thou protect them, do Thou prosper them with victory, do Thou reign over them and rule them as their

Sovereign. Witness my vow, this year of grace, 1640. Thine by piety and by justice,

FERDINAND."

Has not Mary protected the illustrious House of Austria? In the midst of the vicissitudes of greatness, has it not remained the most respected, the most venerated, and the most beloved? May it always remain faithful to Mary! Mary will reward and reciprocate its fidelity.

CHAPTER VIII

Persecutions and Encouragements

WE would astonish even the inattentive reader, if we represented the sodalities of the Blessed Virgin as going through two centuries without meeting the trial of contradiction. He would oppose to us the words of the great Apostle: "All that will live godly in Christ Jesus shall suffer persecution." At least, he would say to us, they were subjected to the annoyances — were a target to the jests of the secular spirit, which piety does not escape and which it conquers easily if it is founded on faith; nay more, it is scarcely possible that they should not have had particular adversaries, if it is true that they instituted so many works of pious zeal, and formed Christians so devoted to the Queen of Heaven.

And, in reality, they were frequently the objects of persecution, and this for several reasons. We shall not dwell on certain local oppositions which do not concern the institution itself; as when F. Claudius Aquaviva had occasion to defend it, in 1596, against the suspicious minds of some ministers of Philip II. at Naples.[1] About the same time, the Grand Duke of Tuscany, Ferdinand I., allowed himself to be imposed upon by calumniators, and imagined that the sodalities of Sienna might endanger the union and equality of the citizens, because they separated the different classes of society, and so he exacted for some time that the nobles should be mixed in them with the people.

There were more formidable enemies. We have seen above that the honor paid to Mary excited the implacable hatred of the heresy that appeared in the sixteenth century; but what is our amazement when, in the seventeenth century, F. Crasset, the director of the sodality at Paris, tells us of certain secret enemies of the Mother of God, who murmured against her devoted children; who devised plausible pretexts of order and regularity to turn the faithful away from the association. Were these heretics, Protestants? No; the pious writer would not have given them the answer which we find in his manual: "It should be enough," he replied, "to represent to them that the Church, to whom alone it belongs to regulate the duties of religion, has established these societies, approved them, enriched them with her favors, and proposed them to the faithful as a

[1] H. S., part V., book XIV., 12.

very suitable means of sanctification." . . . Assuredly the authority of the Sovereign Pontiff little concerned heretics; but to Protestantism there had succeeded, in France and in Belgium, a sect as wicked as it was crafty in concealing itself, of which the adherents, during a century and a half, succeeded, by artifices and even by hypocritical homage, in evading religious authority, and in avoiding an ever-impending condemnation, — we mean the Jansenists. A daughter of the Reformation, she had inherited from her mother a marked aversion for the devotion to Mary. The pretexts that she brought forward to turn aside the faithful from the sodalities, were sometimes the rights of the secular clergy, sometimes the spirit of moderation in the honor paid to the Blessed Virgin.

He must have had eyes covered with a triple bandage of prejudices, who would dare to pretend that, by these pious unions, the Society of Jesus wished to diminish the legitimate authority of a pastor over his flock. Could the Jesuits, whose mission it was so evidently to vindicate the rights of religious authority and of the ecclesiastical hierarchy against the Reformation, be animated by a spirit of division? The numerous priests, whom they saw so assiduous in attending the meetings of the clients of Mary, would never have dreamed of bringing up against them this odious accusation. Their most hostile critics were men imbued with Jansenist principles, and as unfavorable to the devotion of the Blessed Virgin as they were to the privileges of the regular clergy; the few rigorists who, at the end of the seventeenth century, and at the beginning of the eighteenth, harassed the Flemish dioceses, and refused to Mary the title of mediatrix or of Refuge of Sinners, raged against the devotion of the Holy Rosary and the sodalities, and widely disseminated a libel, worthy of Luther, which bore the title: "Salutary Advice of the Blessed Virgin to her Indiscreet Votaries."[1]

At Poitiers, in 1620, the bishop, Henri Chasteignier, a learned and eloquent prelate, saw a storm rising against the regular clergy on the question of parochial rights; he spoke himself with some bitterness against the sodalities, forbidding the Jesuits to receive anyone in them without his authorization. They had no need to lay their cause before the Sovereign Pontiff, from whose decision there could be no appeal. The bishop relented, thanks to the remonstrance of a member of the parliament of Paris, sent by

[1] Cfr. Litt. Ann. -MSC. Coll. Gandav., Archives de l'État à Bruxelles, ad ann. 1674. Records of the English Province, S. J., Foley, XII., p. 210.

the king, and ended by desisting from his demands.[1]

Other difficulties of this kind arose at different places. When, indeed, will calumny or exaggeration cease to throw themselves in the way of good works? On the other hand, we are willing to grant that the zeal on the part of the promoters and directors of the sodalities, cannot always have been free from imprudence and indiscretion. Does this prove anything against the work itself? We could bring forward instances of divine justice with respect to persecutors and slanderers of the sodalities. Father Crasset recounts several, relating, among others, the unhappy death of some sodalists who were unfaithful to their first fervor, and who, after having abandoned the service of the Blessed Virgin, fell into forgetfulness of God and of their duties as Christians. We prefer to omit these details, and to recall facts more important.

Certain parliaments of France rejected those of their members who had been enrolled as children of Mary. But the piety of Louis XIII., anxious to destroy with one stroke several accusations brought against the confraternities and sodalities, issued at Lyons a decree dated October 16, 1630: "It is our wish and pleasure," he said,

[1] H. S. 1620, 93.

"that, in spite of the challenges which we hereby declare frivolous and impertinent, and which we desire to be declared as such by you, you proceed to business without suffering similar ones to be proposed."[1] Sodalities had been formed in France in the garrisoned cities. During a whole century they did not seem to menace danger to the valor of the armies; the old Marshal d'Ornano, Viceroy of Guienne, induced his officers and his men to enroll themselves in them;[2] like Condé and Turenne, he believed that piety was a spur to military courage and the love of duty. After the great reign and the great conquests of Louis XIV., the Jansenist party clamored that the sodalities were a peril to the army. The regent, believing[3] that it was necessary for him to treat the Jansenist reaction with caution, decided that the matter should be brought before the council. In the session of the 19th of July, 1716, the reunions of soldiers presided over by a Jesuit, were interdicted. The Fathers obeyed without demur, and all their sodalities were disbanded. They had conformed without resistance to the orders of authority; but the Jansenists pretended that this compliance was a trick and a

---

[1] Binet, Le Chef d'Œuvre de Dieu. Edition Bouix, p. 538.
[2] Binet, Op. cit. p. 537.
[3] Crétinau-Joly, Histoire de la Compagnie de Jésus.

trap, and they persuaded the regent that his will was evaded. Marshal de Villars, who had consecrated himself to Mary in the confraternity, could not restrain himself from exclaiming: "Who are the rash men that dare to utter such slander? I have in my possession the answers of the generals and governors of our fortifications; all affirm that the orders of the king are strictly fulfilled." Then, addressing himself to his colleagues, he continued: "As for me, gentlemen, I acknowledge, that as long as I have been at the head of our armies, I have never seen soldiers more active, more prompt to execute my orders, more fearless than those who belonged to the sodalities so much accused to-day."

But while Jansenism, encouraged by this first success, pursued with vigor its malicious schemes and its systematic attacks upon the Society of Jesus, the latter received for its work of predilection the reviving encouragements of the Holy See. Aroused by the assaults to which the confraternities were exposed, and by his own experience acquainted with the spirit which animated them, the illustrious Pope Benedict XIV. presented them in 1748 with glorious testimonies. Not content with enriching, them by his bull of April 24, *Præclaris Romanorum*, with new spiritual favors, and in particular with the indulgence of privileged altars, he issued, on the 27th of September, a remarkable bull, which, on account of its importance, had affixed to it the gold seal which the Popes only set on letters of a very solemn character: it is the golden bull *Gloriosæ Dominæ*.

Benedict XIV. begins by praising in magnificent terms the glory of Our Lady, and her titles to the veneration of the faithful. A loving mother, whom the Saviour of the world, in dying, bequeathed to the Church, His spouse; a queen victorious over heresies, a powerful Esther, an invincible Judith, she is besides the mystical ark, the channel of graces and the golden door of Heaven: "Full of these grand thoughts (says the Sovereign Pontiff), Saint Ignatius Loyola ... convinced that he and his new legion would have to engage in severe battles, wisely judged that he could not find more certain help than in the protection of the Blessed Virgin. . . . Therefore it was under her protection that he entered upon the road of perfection; it is at Montmartre, in a chapel consecrated to Holy Mary, that he laid, as on a firm rock, the first foundations of his society. . . . In the same manner, his children, in carrying across the boundless tracts of the land and of the sea the adorable name of Jesus, have not ceased to proclaim at the same time the honey-sweet name of his divine Mother; and with the light of faith and the holiness of morals, have spread in all the countries of the two hemispheres the devotion to Mary, and have given to it a development that approaches the marvellous. Moreover, by a thought inspired by wisdom and realized everywhere, amongst other works of their society, which are all so useful to the church of God, they were active in enrolling youthful Christians in pious sodalities or societies, dedicated to the Blessed Virgin, the Mother of our Redeemer, and they consecrated the faithful to the honor and service of her whom the Holy Ghost calls the Mother of holy affections, of the fear of God, and of true science; thus helping them to walk towards the summit of Christian perfection, and towards the goal of eternal salvation. Thanks to this praiseworthy institution, where the fervor of each particular branch is upheld by wise and pious rules, adapted to the state of life of its members, and carefully maintained by the prudent and enlightened zeal of a director, one can scarcely believe what a salutary influence has been spread throughout all classes of society."

Then, after having displayed the fruits of salvation received from this special devotion to Mary, the great Pontiff continues in these words: "From all that has preceded, it can be plainly seen how wisely inspired were the Roman Pontiffs, our predecessors, in surrounding with their apostolic protection the work of the societies from its very beginning." To the favors granted by Gregory XIII., by Sixtus V., by Clement VIII., and by Gregory XV., he was then pleased to add new ones. " Finally," he says, " We, who, before being raised to Our present dignity, had been inscribed among the number of the members of the sodality in the Professed House at Rome, recall with joy having frequented, for Our greater spiritual consolation, the pious and useful exercises of the sodality of the Assumption. Moreover, judging it to be a duty of Our pastoral ministry to favor and to promote these institutions of solid piety which help to advance in virtue and contribute greatly to the salvation of souls, We have, by our brief of the twenty-fourth of last April, approved, confirmed, and further extended the concessions of Our predecessors. To-day We would even more clearly manifest the interest that We bear for these pious sodalities, in which the religion which man owes to God, and devotion to the Blessed Virgin are practised by means of salutary and praiseworthy works of piety."

With this intention the supreme head of Holy Church permits the sodalities, which have been established in the houses of the Society of Jesus under any title or in honor of any saint, to be affiliated to the Prima Primaria of Rome, and to enjoy its indulgences, on the condition that they take for their principal patroness the Blessed Virgin Mary. He authorizes them, however, to celebrate the feast of their secondary patron, and grants them for that day a plenary indulgence, even in the case of the feast's having been transferred by the Director. The Pontiff then dwells at length on the indulgences, and exhorts the associates to the faithful observance of the rules and to attendance at the meetings. Finally he declares that he cancels, in favor of the sodalities, all that he and Clement VIII. before him had established concerning the method to be followed and the forms to be observed for the foundation of confraternities.

The encouragement given to the work so dear to the sons of Saint Ignatius by the Vicar of Jesus Christ, must have consoled them and animated them with a new ardor in the midst of the signs that foretold the storm which was to break upon them in France and in Spain. Three years after this *bulla aurea*, Benedict XIV. gave a new proof of esteem to the Society of Jesus by the brief, *Quo tibi, dilecte Fili.* It is the first pontifical document in which mention is made of the affiliation of women. The previous bulls did not exclude them; but it had not become a custom to found sodalities of women. Here and there an exception might be noticed; but the Generals of the Society, far from lending a hand, had usually answered attempts of this kind by a refusal of admission.[1] In those days of faith, when human respect had not made so many victims, preference was given to the spiritual direction of men; but Philosophism, with its airs of independence, and its fine words of sovereign reason, and its boast of force of intellect, was about to rule over the higher classes of French society, and soon we shall no longer see the consoling spectacle of great enthusiastic assemblies of the civil authorities, of soldiers, and of gentlemen, begging the honor of ranging themselves under the banner of the supernatural. On the other hand, the share of women in the Christian education of children, and in works of zeal and charity, was to become greater and in some degree to take the place of the influence of men in the world. One might say that the Vicar of Jesus Christ foresaw our new times.

We do not believe that this brief inaugurated many sodalities of women. Jansenism, then in

---

[1] H. S. 1587, 4, — Litt. Ann. 1584, p. 47 — Multæ haud semel, nec una in civitate contenderunt matronæ ut ipsis quoque liceret in hujusmodi convenire cœtus: res nullo modo probata est.

power in France, did not in fact permit it. In 1760 it suppressed all the confraternities; three years later it dispersed the Jesuits. Spain, Portugal, and Naples did the same. The sect remained victorious in its secular struggle against the Society of Jesus. Saint Cyran had written, a century before:[1] " It is of the utmost necessity to ruin the Jesuits if we wish to re-establish the Augustinian doctrine." Its enemies ruined them, but without ruining either truth or the Church.

While the Jansenists and the ministers of the Bourbons, united their forces against the supporters of the throne and the altar, and succeeded in having them exiled from two great Catholic nations, Clement XIII., in his bull *Apostolicum*, took the defence of the society in the name of Holy Church. Nevertheless, his apostolic courage did not save from an almost universal destruction a religious order whose existence might be useful, but was not indispensable, to the preservation of faith. Eight years later the Revolution had the joy of seeing it suppressed by a Pope, who had signed the brief of suppression in spite of himself. The Jesuits respected his misfortunes and fulfilled his orders.

Saint Alphonsus Liguori, who assisted him at his last moments, and who was a witness of the

---

[1] La Secrète Politique des Jansénistes, 1667, p. 210.

remorse of Clement XIV., left his testimony on the question of the sodalities, which we would fain reproduce in finishing this second part of our summary. In a treatise on the Virtues of Mary,[1] he said : " The Sovereign Pontiffs approved them with great praise, and often enriched them with indulgences. Saint Francis de Sales, in his ' Introduction to a Devout Life,' earnestly exhorts secular persons to become members.

"What did Saint Charles Borromeo not do to found and multiply them ? In his synods, he positively directs confessors to urge their penitents to enter them. We ourselves, in the conduct of our missions, have well understood their utility; speaking in general, we find more sins in one man who does not belong to the sodality, than in twenty who are active members."

The Society of Jesus was to disappear everywhere, except in schismatic Russia.

In the next book we shall see whether or not the sodalities shared in their dissolution.

[1] Œuvres Compl.   Paris, 1835, tom. VI. p. 417.

Book III

The Sodalities of the Blessed Virgin in the Nineteenth Century

CHAPTER I

The Sodalities from the Suppression of the Society of Jesus until its Restoration in 1814

IN the great disaster which befel the Society and its apostolic and educational works, it pleased the Divine Goodness to spare the Primary Sodality of the Roman College. For more than a century the piety of its members had been lavish in decorating the chapel of the *Annunziata*. In this sanctuary, which is still admired to-day, the brush of Giacomo Cortese, surnamed Bourguignone, had added to the works of other illustrious artists four masterpieces, representing the great victories of Mary over the enemies of the Christian name.[1] In

---

[1] In memory of the Jubilee of 1884, Father Heijnen has just collected, in an album, photographic reproductions of the striking decorations found in this chapel of the Primaria.

1761, Father Joseph Mazzolari, Director of the Primaria, had obtained for the *Annunziata* an ornament more precious than all the marvels which already decorated it. It was a painting of the Mother of God, from the Catacombs. As early as the pontificate of Clement VIII., it had been detached from a wall in the cemetery of Saint Hermes, and, after having been preserved in the Kircher Museum, was dedicated in the chapel of the *Primaria* by Cardinal Charles Rezzonico; four years later, Cardinal Henry of York, archpriest of the Vatican Basilica, crowned it solemnly. The Holy Virgin, who had been honored in this picture by the martyrs of the first centuries, and who had protected the children of those illustrious Christians, was to see tears flowing from the eyes of the fathers and brothers of the Society of Jesus; but she did not permit the children who had consecrated themselves to her to be dispersed, as were their Directors.[1]

After the suppression, as Father Mazzolari tells us,[2] all that was used for worship was removed from the Roman College; the chapel of the sodality alone remained intact. The Cardinals,

---

[1] Notizie Istoriche e Regole della . . . Prima Primaria, Roma, Salviucci, 1865, p. 13.

[2] Josephi Mariani Parthenii Epistolæ. Rome, MDCCCLXIII; p. 252.

who were entrusted with the dispersion of the Society in Rome, hastened to confide the Primaria to the care of a zealous ecclesiastic, Pietro Antonio Vittene.[1]

Nevertheless, a difficulty soon presented itself in the shape of what the powers of the new director might be. Should he be the successor of the General of the Society in all his rights, and especially in that of aggregating the new sodalities that would be formed? This question presented itself for solution in 1775, *à propos* of the confraternity of merchants of the diocese of Constanza. The Cardinal-Vicar, Marco Antonio Colonna, by letter of May 2, claimed that right for him; but at the Secretariate of Indulgences, objections were raised, and the power of affiliation was limited only to associations of young men who had finished their studies.[2] Some irregular affiliations, as it appears, were made by the want of proper reference to the Ordinary, but these were rectified in July, 1789, by adding the necessary formalities. The zeal of Francis Xavier de Zelada, a former sodalist, and of Settimio Costanzi, the successor of Vittene, obtained a decided gain in 1798.[3] With an extension of his powers that left nothing

---

[1] In the archives of the Primaria is preserved a commentary of his life in manuscript. Proto III. 26.

[2] March 20, 1776, Archives of the Primaria. Proto IV. No 12.

[3] May 5th, Archives of the Primaria, Proto IV., No 22, 23.

more to be desired, the Director of the Primary Sodality was authorized "in future to enroll all the congregations or sodalities of students or of persons of either sex, wherever they were, or wished to be erected."[1]

Another doubt was also removed as to the validity of the privileges formerly accorded to the Generals of the proscribed Society. The confirmation of these privileges was obtained from the Sacred Congregation of Indulgences by the Primaria, on the 6th of March, 1776. Naturally the new decrees mentioned the necessity of securing the consent of the Ordinary; for, since the suppression of the Society, the sodalities forfeited the exemption or immunity which they shared with the Order, and became wholly dependent on the bishops: hence the formula: *de licentia ordinarii.* Besides, for the translation of the feasts of patronage, as well as for the application of indulgences *pro infirmis*, the new summary of indulgences required the consent of the bishop of the place, whereas, the summary of the 7th of December, 1748, only made mention of the Jesuit superiors' permission: *de superiorum suorum licentia.*

---

[1] "Sia transferita al Moderatore della Primaria l'arbitrio e la facoltà d'ascrivere al queste, siano di scolari o di non studenti di qualunque sia sesso ed in qualunque luogo erette o da erigersi." — Notizie Istoriche, p. 11.

On several points, it is easy to see, did the Primaria relax the ancient severity of its statutes. The spirit of poverty had so reflected itself in the rules, that the members were not permitted to come to its aid by any regular collection or expense. The support of the devotion required pecuniary resources, and they had always been provided by the generosity of well-to-do members. In this point and other similar ones, the sodality finally modified its ancient usages, in accordance with the organization of other confraternities. However, the fervor of the members did not diminish. We find a proof of this fervor in the devotion which, as it appears, Settimio Costanzi propagated with a special zeal. A series of rescripts issued from 1798 to 1816, grants them the special permission of celebrating every year in their chapel the proper Mass of the Sacred Heart of Jesus.[1] This devotion, the development of which was especially reserved to our century for the good of a countless number of the faithful, joined itself, in the natural order of things, to the veneration of Mary, as the latter is only a means by which to increase in the love and imitation of our Lord: for we cannot attach ourselves to this Divine Mother without at the same time attaching ourselves more closely to her Divine Son. This

[1] Archives of the Primaria, proto N° 25, 30.

principle, which is fundamental in the devotion to Mary, must later have been that which inspired F. Fava (director of the Primaria in 1864), with the idea of forming a pious union against the blasphemies of which our Blessed Lord is the object. Pius IX. was pleased to approve it, and to attach it canonically to the sodality, by his brief of Dec. 20, 1867, *Maximas inter angustias*.[1]

But while the Primary Sodality, the centre of all those found in the Catholic world, was sustained by the zeal of Vittene and Costanzi, outside of Rome the work suffered severely from the dispersion of the Society of Jesus. Here and there, devout priests made efforts to maintain these pious unions: we are permitted, at least, so to believe from the testimony of copies of the rules, printed at Ingolstadt in Bavaria, Saint-Brieuc in France, at Bergamo, Venice, Brussels, and elsewhere.[2] The sodalities of Fribourg, that had been so efficient, happily sustained themselves throughout the revolutionary period, under the direction of former Jesuits, until the time

[1] Direttorio della pia unione contra la bestemmia ed il parlare osceno. Roma, Marini, 18º, 288 pp.

[2] Ingolstadt, 1775. Leges et statuta cum variis precibus ac exercitiis congregationis B. Virginis Mariæ, 16º. Heures de Saint-Brieuc à l'usage des congréganistes, 1780. — Regole e statuti della congregazione. Bergame, 1795, item Venezia, 1802. — Association en faveur des congréganistes de la Ste. Vierge, Bruxelles, 1780.

when the Society was able to resume its labors in that city. The same thing occurred in the cities of Cologne, Aix-la-Chapelle, and a few others. In Namur[1] the Recollect Fathers took charge of and held in their convent the meetings of the sodality of the Immaculate Conception. After 1796, Father Norbert, a Capuchin, and Father Donat, of the Recollects, occasionally called meetings of the members in different quarters of the city. But with the loss of the colleges of the Society, the greater number of the sodalities lost their place of reunion: and even those that reorganized themselves, were hardly able to resist the trials that the clergy had to endure: the times became worse and worse, and the tempest that raged against altar and throne was felt in every Catholic land.

In the midst of the general uprooting that began with the suppression of the Society of Jesus, the sodalities of Bavaria supposed themselves suppressed with it; but the prince-elector of the duchy wished to preserve them. Being himself a member of one of them, he appreciated their usefulness for works of piety and mercy; and by an autograph letter addressed to the Provincial of Bavaria on the 22d of June, 1771, had acknowledged the services rendered by them dur-

---

[1] Congrégation de jeunes hommes de Namur. Précis historiques, 1864.

ing the famine of the preceding year, and had thanked the Jesuits for the zeal and edification shown by them in their devotion to his subjects. He likewise wrote to Pope Clement XIV., and obtained[1] in April 1774, a brief in which the eight sodalities of the diocese of Freisingen were not only confirmed, but enriched with new indulgences. But for all that they were not spared from severe trials during the revolution and the wars of Napoleon: in 1802 the Baron de Montgelas, minister to Maximilian IV., commenced the work of secularization. The splendid sodality of Munich was among its first victims. Dispossessed of its wealth and of its place of meeting (which has been recently restored), it was removed to the church of the Holy Trinity.[2] In 1813, though greatly fallen from its ancient prosperity, this sodality numbered 575 ecclesiastics, and 655 laymen.

By a wonderful dispensation of Providence, the sons of Loyola, banished by Catholic princes, and sacrificed by the hand of Clement XIV., found a shelter in schismatic Russia. Catherine II., with a view of averting the complete destruction of the Society, prevented the pontifical brief from taking

---

[1] Feller, Historical and Literary Journal, 1775. I. p. 439.

[2] Sattler, Geschichte der Marianischen Congregationen in Bayern, pages 166, 177, et seq.

effect in her vast empire: she even prohibited its publication. This step, it is said, did not displease the Sovereign Pontiff; soon after, Pius VI. issued a letter, Aug. 15, 1778, allowing the Jesuits of White Russia to open a novitiate.[1] In the six colleges directed by the Society of Jesus in 1784,[2] the sodalities of the Blessed Virgin held the traditional place which had always been theirs in the work of Christian education. In Polotz a manual was published for their use.[3]

The English Jesuits of Saint Omer, after having been successively banished from France in 1763, from the Low Countries in 1773, and from Liége in 1794, found an assured refuge in their own country. The sodality of Stonyhurst justly prides itself on having surmounted the difficulties of the suppression, and of having had an uninterrupted existence since 1617, as is proved by a document in its possession.[4] We have touching testimony of the zeal displayed by the fervent English sodalists for the conversion of their country. "Jesus, Jesus, convert England, *fiat, fiat!*" are the words which they repeat each day, and which we

---

[1] Feller, Journal historique, 1785, vol. III. p. 280.

[2] Ditto, 1784, vol. II. p. 191.

[3] Polociæ 1794. Leges et statuta congregationum B. Virginis.

[4] Pietas Mariana Britannica, by Edmund Waterton, F. S. A., Knight of the Order of Christ, p. 101. . . . Memorials of Stonyhurst College, London, Burns & Oates, 1881, pp. 11, 40.

find inscribed in the chapel of their country-house at Chévremont. They have at last found a footing in that dower-land of Mary's, where the dawn of religious liberty had at last appeared, and where their prayers, and those of their successors, will undoubtedly hasten the full, bright day of Catholic faith: *fiat, fiat!* How many are the descendants of noble families and of martyrs who have inscribed their illustrious names in the registers of this sodality under the title of "Servus Perpetuus Beatæ Mariæ Virginis." "It is with joy and consolation," wrote the author of the *Pietas Mariana Britannica* some years ago, "that I recall those happy days when I was a sodalist at Stonyhurst. The chanting of the 'Hours of the Immaculate Conception' seemed to me more full of melody than anything that has since reached my ears: could it have been that those who sang were '*innocentes manibus et mundo corde?*'—'unstained of hand and clean of heart.' Many have been the years gone by, many the friends that have died whose lips, now closed, once sang with me the praises of Mary, and nevertheless, even as I write these lines, an echo of what Dante calls 'the soft accents of psalmody,' still rings in my heart. How sweet will be the remembrance of the day of consecration to Mary, when at the last hour will appear in the Book of Life that pure and bright page on which will be inscribed our act of consecration! When after having repeated it daily, when after having lived as worthy children of Mary, what will not the peace of our souls be when with a feeble voice, but still with a stout English heart, we shall say for the last time:—

> "'Maria, mater gratiæ,
> Mater misericordiæ,
> Tu nos ab hoste protege
> Et mortis hora suscipe.'"

In the beginning of this century, a few faithful servants of Our Lady made use of the return of peace to reorganize the sodalities, but this reorganization was not always canonical: without direct connection with the Primaria of Rome, and without a new diploma of affiliation, the privileges granted by the Sovereign Pontiffs could not be enjoyed. The greater number of them finally did enjoy these privileges by securing a diploma when the Jesuits reopened their colleges. We have obtained the exact number of those who were thus affiliated between the years 1800 and 1824, when the direction of these sodalities was held by the Jesuits; 135 in Italy, 8 in France, and 2 in England.[1]

[1] Archives of the Primaria, Congregazioni aggregate, proto VIII.

Let us borrow from Father Guidée[1] a few details connected with the attempt of the restoration of the sodalities in France, and with this extract we shall have exhausted the subject of this chapter.

Father Jean Baptiste Delpuits, formerly a Jesuit, was graciously received by the Archbishop of Paris, Mgr. de Beaumont, and offered a canonship in the collegiate church of the Saint-Sépulcre. After the Reign of Terror, this man of God, having before his eyes the spectacle of youths almost entirely deprived of spiritual assistance, conceived the idea of establishing a sodality. Six students of law and medicine, Buisson and Fiseau, Regnier, de Marignan, Mathieu and Eugène de Montmorency, composed the first nucleus. Cardinal De Bellay, then Archbishop of Paris, approved and gave his blessing to the work, which, considering the license and impiousness of the age, in a short time attained an extraordinary success. These young men, untainted by the spirit of their age, and strengthened by the teachings of their venerable director, visited the hospitals which were deprived of the ministrations of religion, and used their influence in regaining

---

[1] Notices historiques sur quelques membres de la Société des Pères du Sacré Cœur et de la Compagnie de Jésus, tome II, pp. 22, 68.

their companions to regular habits, and especially in protecting from vice those newly arrived from the provinces. In the course of a few years, Father Delpuits could count in his sodality members who were later destined to honor the ranks of the episcopate, the peerage, the army, the forum and the field of science.

In September, 1809, he had the great sorrow of seeing the meetings discontinued on account of a cloud in the political sky; several members were arrested on the charge of having distributed divers briefs of the Sovereign Pontiff, Pius VII. He died in 1811, on the octave of the Immaculate Conception. His children in Christ erected to his memory a modest tomb with this inscription:

R. P. J. B. DELPVITS · SOC JESV · PRESBYTER DEO · DEVOTOS · AC · DEIPARÆ · VIRGINI INNVMEROS · VERBO · ET · EXEMPLO · ALVMNOS INFORMAVIT

The work of the zealous priest, who, in the midst of this sad epoch, was able to form many servants of Mary, was not destined to die with him. Philibert de Bruyard, later on Bishop of Grenoble, reunited its scattered members in 1814, and the Abbé Legris-Duval presided over their meetings in the private chapel of the seminary of Foreign Missions.

CHAPTER II

The Extension of the Sodalities since 1814

THERE was rejoicing in the city of Rome, Cardinal Pacca tells us in his memoirs, when, on the 7th of August, 1814, Pope Pius VII. went to the church of the Gesù, and there published the bull for the re-establishment of the Society of Jesus. "The Catholic world unanimously demands," said the Holy Father, "that the Society be re-established; we daily receive letters to that effect from our venerable brothers, the bishops. Placed as we are at the helm of the bark of Peter, we cannot refuse the offer that Providence makes us of these experienced oarsmen."

The bull *Sollicitudo omnium ecclesiarum* recommends the surviving members of the Society and its new sons, to the protection of the princes of Holy Church and to sovereigns. Five hundred and fifty members of the society, who came from England, Russia, and the Low Countries, had the consolation of assisting at this ceremony, and to see realized a hope that not even the greatest calamities of the time had ever been able to quench.

The Superior General of the order was unable to leave Russia, where for the last ten years he had governed the small band of the sons of Loyola. It was not until 1820 that his successor, Aloysius Fortis, established his residence in Rome. Four years later, Leo XI. gave back to the Society the direction of the Roman College and of the Oratory of Caravita, and at the same time reinstated it in all the rights over the sodalities previously conceded it by the Holy See. This was the object of the brief, *Cum multa in Urbe*, issued on May 17, 1824. After recalling all that the society had done both in the field of letters and of piety, he surrendered to it the direction of the Roman College and all its dependencies. "It is Our desire," added the Sovereign Pontiff, "that they should exert themselves in instructing and forming to virtue young men through the sodalities, as well as that they should care for the faithful who frequent their oratory. To this effect We decree that the Roman College be returned to them in all its integrity, and notably the right of conferring degrees in the arts and in theology, which was conceded them by the letters apostolic of Julius III. and of Pius IV., and also the right of aggregating new foundations to the sodality of the Annunciation, known as the Prima Primaria." [1]

It was therefore after an interruption of fifty years that the Society of Jesus undertook again in Rome the work of the sodalities. This work, however, entered upon a new era. Until now it had been confined exclusively to the houses of the Society and to the oratories dependent on it; moreover, only associations of men and boys had been comprised. Under these two heads a radical change took place, especially during the ten years that elapsed between the decree of the reestablishment and the brief of 1824. In fact, during these ten years the sons of St. Ignatius, finding themselves in numbers too small to found many colleges, and desirous, nevertheless, to see the sodalities of Our Lady revived, had given encouragement to those that had sustained themselves, and lent an active hand to the foundation of other sodalities, parishes, and in seminaries. Some of these had been erected without the intervention even of the director of the Prima Primaria.

Father Aloysius Fortis, in order to put an end to

[1] Jura porro ac privilegia Collegii romani, illaque præsertius quibus ex Julii III. et Pii IV. auctoritate, lauream in artibus et in sacræ theologiæ facultate impertiri, pariterque congregationi Annunciationis B. M. V., Primæ Primariæ nuncupatæ, aggregare datum est, integre perstare decernimus.

certain doubts that might suggest themselves as regarded these defective foundations, addressed a request to the Vicar of Jesus Christ, and in a private audience the Holy Father was pleased to grant him, on March 7, 1825, all the necessary powers to aggregate all the sodalities that were not directed by the Society, and that might ask to be so aggregated. This favor, though it in no way lessened the rights of the episcopacy over the foundation or erection of any association founded within the limits of their jurisdiction, was so considerable that at first sight it appeared in opposition to the decree of Clement VIII. It might have been put in doubt had the terms of both the petition and the answer not been couched in the clearest language;[1] moreover, the privilege was

---

[1] The petition was couched in these terms: "Luigi Fortis, prega vostra Beatitudine di poter aggregare alla Prima Primaria tutte le altre Congregazioni che non sono dirette dalla Compagnia, che il richiedissero, rendendosi in tal guisa la Pontificia grazia comprehensiva di tutte le congregazioni, come fu nel 5 maggio 1798, conceduta al Direttore pro tempore della prælodota Congregazione con benigno rescritto del sommo Pontifice Pio VI di s. m. que chi si umilia et come fu fino a questi ultimi tempi praticato dai respettivi Direttori della Prima Primaria."

Ex audientia SSmi, die 7 martii 1825.

SSmus, attentis expositis, remisit preces arbitrio ejusdem oratoris P. Præp. Gen. Soc. Jesu cum omnibus facultatibus necessariis et opportunis. Contrariis quibuscumque non obstantibus. —(Card. Guerrieri.)

These documents are preserved at the Professed House at Rome.

again and again confirmed. As we have said above, the Prima Primaria differs essentially from any other association or confraternity; it suffers no application of the bull *Quæcumque.* On Jan. 8, 1861, the Sacred Congregation of Indulgences, anxious to recall to the confraternities the terms of this bull, issued a memorable decree in such express clauses that doubts arose as to the continuance of the Primaria in preserving her prerogatives. The very Reverend Father Becks submitted these doubts to the Congregation of Indulgences, and the latter declared, on Aug. 29, 1864, that the sodalities of the Blessed Virgin were not comprised in this decree.[1]

Such facilities granted for the erection of sodalities, together with the numerous privileges enjoyed by persons of both sexes and all ages, produced the happiest results; the affiliations became very numerous; their number would need explanation did one not know how much the devotion to the Blessed Mother of God has increased in this century, thanks to the zeal of the clergy, whose principal aim seems to have been to extend the veneration of Mary. It is, above all, due to the honor of the episcopacy that they have encouraged this devotion to the extent of having, through this means, prepared the way for the

[1] Cf. Acta S. Sedis, vol. II. p. 29.

triumphs enjoyed by Holy Church. Will not our century be ever called the century of the glories of Mary, the century of the Immaculate Conception?

During the first two hundred and forty years of the association, that is to say, from 1584 to 1824, the number of diplomas of affiliation issued by the Primaria amounted to 2476. During the next forty years, 7040 were issued. It is worthy of notice that a surprising number of these sodalities were erected in honor of the Immaculate Conception; from 1824 to 1833 we have counted no less than 130: moreover in 1832, thirty more were founded under the title of "The Immaculate Heart of Mary."[1] We thus see that, long before the dogmatic definition of the great privilege of the Virgin Mother, it was loudly affirmed by the faith of the Catholic universe, and that to this period in particular do the words of the bull *Ineffabilis Deus* apply: "It is this doctrine, so ancient, and so well engraved in the heart, that the whole world has propagated, thanks to the ardor and zeal of the bishops; and it is this doctrine that has been approved by the Church when she proposed to the devotion of all the faithful the feast of the Immaculate Conception."

Let us here remind the associates that it was in

[1] Archives of the Primaria. Prot º VIII., IX.

this same bull, that Pius IX., of glorious memory, was pleased to make mention of the sodalities :—
"Our predecessors held it ever to be their great honor, that they might promote in every possible way, homage to the Immaculate Virgin, be it by allowing cities, provinces, and kingdoms to take as their patroness the Mother of God, under the title of the Immaculate Conception, be it in approving that sodalities, confraternities, and families of religious should be established in honor of this prerogative."

In the rapid extension of the work of the sodalities, we should not overlook the fact of the superior number of those erected for women. A few simple reflections will suffice to explain the zeal with which they were multiplied, as also the readiness on the part of the Primaria to accord to them the privilege of affiliation.

In the society of the seventeenth, and even of the eighteenth century, there still reigned a spirit that was essentially Christian. In the social relations, as well as in the bosom of the family, the faith was held in honor, and morals were simple and severe : daughters were brought up with little or no contact with the world, and they carried into their own homes, the habits of retirement and modesty taught them by their parents. Young women were not then exposed to the numerous dangers that now assail virtue and purity in our large cities. Social festivities and entertainments were much rarer than at present, and of a much more wholesome kind. Especially in villages and small towns certain kinds of amusements were wholly unknown, which to-day cause great anxiety and solicitude to parents and religious authorities. From different points of view, as it is well known, the situation of things in our day is very different. How natural it becomes, therefore, to resort to new means of piety and virtue in order to meet new dangers.

Besides the superior attraction that pleasure may have for the sex, other considerations belonging to our time have combined to make it desirable also to unite women in confraternities and sodalities. Indeed, how many are the charitable associations that have risen in our day! associations that might have before been deemed unnecessary, or, at least, much less necessary; and would these charities support themselves and be spread without the aid of a religious centre? Moreover, it is well known how great has become the religious influence of women in these days of indifference on the part of the sex that should have been the directing influence of our societies. There is not to be found a Christian orator of the first half of our century, who does not bemoan the degeneracy of character and the weakening of soul. The older generation of the present time had their convictions influenced by a rampant spirit of incredulity, and their resistance shaken by human respect. Moreover, we may allow ourselves to apply to the women of to-day what Montalembert said of virgins consecrated to the Lord : " In this age of great pusillanimity and of universal religious indifference, these victorious ones become the guardians of the secret of strength, and, in the very weakness of their sex, show forth the virility and persevering energy so sadly lacking in ours, yet without which it is impossible to oppose the sensuality, the egotism, the baseness of our times.[1] Must we not indeed acknowledge that, during a certain period, both in France and in Belgium, it would have been difficult to maintain, and much less to found, any work of religion or charity composed of men alone? Religious instruction for them was scarcely tolerated : it became necessary, whilst awaiting a new generation of men, of Christians, to throw the weight of Christian works on those who had always been called the weaker sex. The part that women were destined to play, became more important ; it was not, therefore, surprising, that sodalities for them should multiply from this time forward.

[1] Works in 8vo, vol. V., p. 375.

Without entering into all the details of this development, let us merely cite a few facts that will go to prove the wisdom of admitting women into the confraternities. We regret that we must limit the present subject to a narrow space; for a whole volume would hardly do justice to the matter before us. In 1816, in the city of Saint-Brieuc, after a very successful mission that was preached there, a sodality of young women was founded there by the Abbé Fr. Renault,[1] a professor in the seminary of that city. Not satisfied with having their Sunday reunions, these young persons, whose position in life allowed them some leisure, devoted themselves to the instruction of poor children, and their piety soon discovered to them, in the exercise of this work of mercy, the joys of the religious life. The little community of Sisters of Providence was born in their midst. It was founded by the Abbé Jean Maria de Lamennais; it opened several houses and is still in existence. Might not one assign a similar birth to several of these fervent sodalities of religious that our time has seen multiplying themselves in every diocese of France and of Belgium? And were these not in many instances founded by these very women, who, under the in-

---

[1] Notice Historique sur le P. Fr. Renault, par Ach. Guido, p. 19.

spiration of a priest led by the Spirit of God, were devoted daughters of the Blessed Virgin? Many of them have, indeed, become instruments of sanctification, and the means by which the faith in many of our cities has been preserved and developed.

In 1835, the city of Alost had a flourishing sodality of young women, many of whom showed extraordinary firmness in resisting pleasures, public amusements, and festivities. They celebrated the Lord's Day in a truly Christian spirit, giving their spare hours to the instruction of the poor children in the Sunday schools. All the cities of Belgium, since the liberties gained in 1830, have established such schools, largely with the help of the sodalists.

In 1836, while the agents of Bible Societies were actively employed in spreading broadcast books that might prove dangerous to the faith of our population, the members of the sodalities distinguished themselves for the zeal they displayed in counteracting this influence, even to buying from the hands of the poor the obnoxious literature. The sodality of young ladies counted then about one hundred and forty members, and that of the working girls, three hundred. The Bishop of Ghent, Louis Delebecque, would often honor the meetings with his presence.

It was thus that the canon of Montpellier, afterwards bishop of Liège, expressed himself in the ninth chapter of the manual he edited for the use of the ladies at Namur.[1] "The sodality has for its object not only the sanctification of its members, but also the procuring of the welfare of their neighbor, by the different works that Christian charity and true piety may inspire; each section may follow its own inclination in the choice of a work, each participating in all the works of the whole sodality. There are three sections: 1st, that of the poor; 2d, that of the work-room, and 3d, that of the house of God. Each section has its president, secretary, and treasurer. These should always act in common consent with the president of the whole association, and take her advice. Charity to the poor shall be exercised, through almsgiving, visits, counsel, and so forth. The work-room is under the direction of the sodalists: they receive poor workmen and shield them from corrupting influences; they furnish work; they watch over their morals. Those members whose tastes do not lead them to exterior good works can utilize both time and means by furnishing for poor churches all the articles necessary for divine worship."

[1] Livre de prières à l'usage des dames associées aux congregations de la Sainte Vièrge. D. Namur, F. J. Dourfils, in 18, 412 pp.

In 1841 some lady sodalists in Louvain began a charitable work in favor of poor laborers, under the direction of the Vice-rector of the University. They made garments which they afterwards distributed in the homes of the workmen, and there often discovered spiritual necessities that were even greater, and in which they lent their assistance. In 1843 they had decided to unite them on Sundays for spiritual instruction, in the chapel of St. Anthony: at first about twenty workmen attended, but before Easter their number arose to three hundred. During the first years many opportunities were found to legitimatize marriages, to bring to the holy table unhappy sinners, to extricate their whole families from vice, and from the consequences of extreme poverty. A scholastic of the Society of Jesus gave them instruction once a week. To this day, thanks to so much zeal, the work has not ceased to bear fruit in abundance; once a year, under the presidency of the Vice-rector of the University, and of the rector of the Jesuit College, the ladies make a generous distribution of clothing, discriminating among those more worthy of their bounty.[1]

The young ladies' sodalities of the same town are in a most flourishing condition. When the rates of interment into the Catholic cemeteries

[1] Litt. Ann. Prov. Belg. 1843, p. 24.

became burdensome to poor families on account of the taxes imposed by the Liberal administration, one of the sodalities started a society for mutual assistance, in order that the members might enjoy Christian burial. Several missionary institutions exist in Louvain, in which the ladies take an active and infinitely useful interest: we need only mention the Sunday-school for poor girls and the Apostolic work-rooms. To procure for the students of the Apostolic school, clothing and other materials for their long studies, and afterwards to render their entrance into a religious order or into the seminary for foreign missions feasible, is the object towards which these hand-maidens truly devoted to the service of Mary consecrate a part of their money and their leisure. Similar works are established in many other sodalities.

Country parishes have accepted female sodalities with no less favor. In one year alone more than forty were founded.[1] The following lines we translate from a letter written by a curé: "During the last Jubilee I had the pleasure of helping some of my colleagues, and I can safely state that in the parishes where women's sodalities exist, there are more modesty, better morals, and a more solid piety. Though I have not spared any effort

---

[1] Litt. Ann. Prov. Belg. 1853. p. 11.

in the thirteen years that I have spent here, I must allow that my parish is inferior in respect to piety and morals to that of many of my colleagues. I therefore propose to establish a confraternity of the Blessed Virgin." Among the most efficacious means resorted to by pastors, we recommend this one: During the week of the *kermesse* the sodality furnishes the opportunity of making the annual retreat; the less edifying of the members at once refuse to join in these pious exercises, thereby adding to the recollection and fervor with which they are carried out; the more courageous inscribe their names and so escape the temptations and dangers that are sure to attend worldly pleasures.

If we thus speak principally of Belgium, it is because the situation there is best known to us; moreover, an advantage has been enjoyed there that other Catholic countries may well envy; fifty years of a peace that, though often menaced, has not been entirely broken, have made it possible to strengthen and develop religious societies. A great element of prosperity is to be found in the character of the Belgian clergy, whose praises it is needless here to repeat; hence the number of sodalists is comparatively greater than elsewhere.

It is worthy of notice that of the seven thousand diplomas of affiliation issued by the Prima Primaria and extended all over the world in the last forty years, Catholic Belgium has claimed nearly two thousand. Must we not, therefore, seek in these confraternities the secret of a part at least, if not of the entire progress made by faith and piety in this country? For, far from denying the power of the enemies of our religion and of their skepticism, it is only just to acknowledge that, thanks to the faithful children of the church, and thanks above all to the frequentation of the sacraments, piety and the true Christian spirit are making great progress in our midst.

We would make this chapter too long, were we to trace the history of the sodalities of the Children of Mary. All those who have read the life of F. de Ravignan will know the good they have wrought in souls, and the magnificent work in the midst of the world that owes to them its birth and accomplishment.[1] In the education of young ladies, special devotion to Mary has produced similar results to those witnessed in the colleges for youths. Under wise and safe direction the privileged Children of Mary attain to the exercise

[1] The Sodality of the Children of Mary, erected in the convent of the Sacred Heart of Jesus, at the Trinita de' Monti, in Rome, was affiliated to the Prima Primaria of the Roman College, Jan. 7, 1837. — Regole della Congregazione delle Figlie di Maria che vivono in mezzo al secolo. Roma, typ. A. Monaldi, 1844, p. 21.

of the highest virtues, and they compose in the midst of their companions a centre of piety and of Christian edification. By their modesty, their zeal, and their attachment to their teachers, they co-operate in a great measure with the work of education. The Ladies of the Sacred Heart, the Sisters of Notre Dame, and those of Sainte Marie, and many other flourishing institutes, are daily gathering fruits of virtue through the influence of the sodalities of the Blessed Virgin. These are, so to speak, the soul of their academies.

CHAPTER III

Sodalities of Students

WHAT a beautiful subject is here presented to our pen! It is almost impossible to resist the pleasure of treating it; but the matter is inexhaustible, and when these large and fervent associations of children and of young men present themselves in brilliant array before us, we hesitate, lest we might fail to do justice to traits of virtue that, in never-ending succession, are rejoicing the heart of the Queen of Angels, and honoring the sodalities of our colleges and academies. We shall be unable even to mention the most pious amongst them. Shall we, therefore, confine ourselves only to a few generalities which will apply in a greater or less degree to them all? No; let us try to do justice to all by putting before us one organization, that of Saint-Acheul, and we cannot do better than to introduce a resumé of an excellent little volume,[1] that all

---

[1] La Congrégation de la T. S. Vièrge à Saint-Acheul, par le R. P. Charles Clair. Paris, Baltenweck, 1877, 180, 220 pages.

directors of these associations of students should read in order to penetrate into the true spirit which should guide these assemblies.

In October, 1814, Father Clorivière, a member of the old Society of Jesus, reopened the college of Saint-Acheul, and received into the order Father Louis de Bussi; this young priest was the first director of the sodality.[1] His name is generally best known in connection with his book, "The Month of Mary," so celebrated and so beloved of all Christian souls. Through this book, so many times reprinted, and containing such admirable doctrines, he made many conversions and greatly aided in propagating the salutary custom of keeping the month of May as consecrated to the Blessed Virgin. For seven years he devoted himself to his beloved confraternity of students with a zeal that was full of amiability, as well as of prudence. It was thought well to admit only thirty-three pupils at the first reception, and the greatest care was afterwards taken in the admission of subsequent members. The postulants had first to present themselves to one of the three principal officers, and through them to the father director. They had repeatedly to request admission, and generously to agree to all the conditions, the chief of which resumed them all,

---

[1] Guide, Notice, II., 249, 303.

viz., uniform good conduct and application. After the first term of probation, which might be extended to several months, they were admitted as *approved* members and might attend the morning meetings, which were of a devotional character. With the advice of the consulters, after a fresh probation, also to last for an indefinite time, the director would appoint the day for their solemn reception. It was not all to have succeeded in entering the sodality; a student had to show himself worthy of *remaining* a member. If he violated or neglected the promise made on the day of consecration, the delinquent was only admonished or deprived for a time of the right of attendance, according to the gravity of the offence. Sometimes it was judged necessary to make these admonitions more public and impressive. We will now pass on to different works of charity undertaken by each section, making only a passing mention of the pious practices in use in this sodality. One was the drawing for a monthly patron among the saints; another was the gift of a little pious sketch distributed by the director as a souvenir to the pupils; still another was the short morning meditation to be voluntarily made each day, which was apart from the daily routine of the school. Father Bussi had the faculty of extending to its utmost capacity the usefulness of the charities performed. He would divide the members into groups, so as to give those that composed it the work which was best suited to their tastes and capacities. The first group or section cared for the necessities, both spiritual and corporal, of the *sick and the imprisoned;* facilities for visiting these classes were afforded them, just as at present some sodalities have access to the old people in the homes of the Little Sisters of the Poor. The second section cared for the *poor*, and distributed to them food and money; at the same time they would ask them simple questions from the catechism, and teach their prayers to those amongst them who were wholly ignorant, thus giving them both spiritual and bodily assistance. There is an indigence of spirit which is even worse than destitution of body, and the sight of boys recalling to men bowed down by age and infirmity the truths of the faith and the duties of religion, could not but bring reverently to our minds, Jesus preaching in the temple at the age of twelve.

The duties of the section of the *Sanctuary*, are sufficiently explained by its title. To embellish the altar of Mary, to adorn it for her principal festivals, and to maintain the neatness and decorum of the sanctuary, are the occupations of the members of the section. Last, but not least, F.

Bussi organized the section of *zeal:* here were consecrated the principal efforts made in the direction of this virtue, though it was one that all the pupils, without distinction, were expected to practise. As there is nothing that has so vast a field as zeal, three subdivisions were made: in the first, arguments were presented with the view of fortifying Catholic convictions, and of showing the fallacy of certain current sophisms; the debaters, over whom the director presided, were thus able to strenghthen themselves in true principles. In the second subdivision, by being full of zeal for the honor of the Mother of God, the members tried to render her the most tender homage, and to propagate her veneration and devotion; it was an apostleship of Mary, practised with discretion by young and ardent hearts. The end of the third subdivision was to render assistance to the newcomers among the students. There is something truly pathetic in the situation of a boy who for the first time leaves the parental roof for the life of a large boarding-school. At best he can only meet with indifference on the part of his comrades: he feels quite alone in the little world that surrounds him, and his thoughts fly back to the absent family circle, while his heart is filled with longing, sadness, and discouragement. If a charitable schoolfellow approaches him in order that he may do him some of those innumerable little services that are so acceptable under the circumstances; if he makes him feel at home; if he stands by him in the trials and difficulties of the first few weeks, — he will undoubtedly have filled towards him a noble position, and will have spared him many an hour of low spirits that, as the Scriptures tell us, cannot but bring evil consequences. Such was the task allotted to this third subdivision. Charitable devices, delicate ingenuity, little services and consolations, nothing was neglected, and very soon a single word about the sodality, and the happiness of belonging to it, would bring one more loving child of Mary to the feet of his Mother.

A spirit of good will and of piety, — this only is needed to transform a school into a truly christian home. The sodality is the centre of piety, and from it is to come that spirit of good will on which is based every virtue that is to bear fruit in an educational establishment. Mary, the Mother and Patroness of the Sodality, found in these young souls the sentiments of the tenderest devotion.

When some more solemn festival presented itself; or if the month of May invited the pupils to honor their Mother with still heartier devotion, neither flowers nor lights were spared. Piety received a fresh impulse; some new practice was suggested, and often, for greater honor to the Month of their Queen, it was decided that several members should daily approach the Holy Table in the name of all, while others should unite with them in spirit and prayer.

Jesus and Mary, closely bound to each other during their earthly lives, are still united together in the devotion of the faithful, in whose hearts they cannot be separated. Devotion to the Sacred Heart was in its fullest fervor in the sodality. Its members clung to the cultus of reparation paid to the Son of God. If there is one practice which the Saviour recommended more than another, to the interpreter of His wishes, the B. Margaret Mary, it is that of Communion on the first Friday of the month. The associates were eager to comply with the Saviour's request. Often, on the first Friday of the month, more than three hundred young men might be seen assembled in church for the purpose of bestowing this mark of their love and respect upon Jesus.

When piety is alive, all else lives, especially the spirit of duty. What duty is there more important to a student than that of his studies? The thought of Mary guided our associates in their literary pursuit. Those upon whom our Lord had not lavished gifts of intellect gave themselves up, for her sake, to the most laborious application, without flagging or discouragement. Others, more favored intellectually, found, in their Mother's love, an incentive to the development of their talents. The spirit of humility and obedience, went hand in hand with industry. Doubtless, at Saint Acheul, as everywhere, human nature was weak and subject to failure; but when a fault was committed, not only was reparation witnessed, but it was often spontaneous.

Serious insubordinations did not occur. There was no unseemly pride in success; no vainglory over a generous act. It once happened that a lad of fourteen gave quite a considerable sum in alms to a little Savoyard. He thought he was unobserved. But in the evening, the Father Prefect of discipline, who had witnessed the act, related it to the pupils, without, of course, mentioning the benefactor's name. At once the boy tried to turn the conversation; still the Father continued. The poor boy blushed, was embarrassed, and, finding his efforts useless, at last burst into tears. Nothing could console him but leaving the story unfinished. The next day, however, his secret having been told, his tears and entreaties were understood.

Humility is not weakness, and the humility of the members was as far removed from human respect as it was from pride.

Two children were in the house of a stranger where the Church's abstinence was not observed. They said to each other: "We will not commit a mortal sin through cowardice." As they left untouched the dishes which were offered to them, they were questioned, and urged to eat. Finally, they referred to ·the commandments of the Church. Entreaties, old worldly maxims by which men persuade themselves that in society they may cease to be Christians,— all were in vain, and the generous courage of the children prevailed.

If the members of the sodality, on leaving college, are grounded in solid principles, and are strong in virtue, why should it be astonishing that they carry a lively and zealous faith with them into the world? Why should not the thoughts of these youths go back to those sacred walls, where under the shadow of Mary's sanctuary, they were trained in the Christian life? Or, why should they not frequently return to that refuge to renew their strength and reanimate their courage, by living again the old life?

Each member found piety, encouragement to virtue, and strength to practise a good life, in the sodality. Besides, each one understood that, to please Mary, he must pour out upon others the abundance of his charity and devotion. *Cor unum et anima una* — one heart and one soul — was the keynote animating and harmonizing the thoughts and sentiments of the associates, under the protection of their Mother. Their hearts were large enough to embrace all of their companions without preference or exclusion. A trying temper, an obstinate disposition, were not a sufficient excuse for depriving a youth of the love of his schoolfellows. On the contrary, love ingeniously courted cold or rebellious hearts in the hope of drawing out their better side.

Prudence was the only limit to such love. Sometimes a member was obliged to practise the precept, *Prima sibi caritas* — "Charity begins at home." With rare exceptions, concord, peace, joy, a good understanding, were the rule at Saint Acheul; charity within being only equalled by that which was diffused without. The college courtyard, to which the poor flocked, attics, cabins, schools, prisons, hospitals, were so many fields for our associates. St. Vincent de Paul, that great friend and helper of the indigent, had been given as the second patron to the division for the poor. The pupils strove to imitate their perfect model, and offered special prayers daily to obtain the spirit which should guide their humble ministry. We must see our Lord Jesus Christ in the poor. If the poor are always with us, it is because Jesus would immortalize in His Church the memory of His poverty, and perpetuate His own apostolate towards those who have no earthly inheritance. Were not the members serving the Son of God when, on Holy Thursday, prostrating themselves at the feet of the poor, they did not blush to perform that humble service of which noble and Christian princes have not been ashamed?

In like manner these young pupils initiated themselves in the spirit of self-sacrifice, renouncing pleasure to relieve misfortune. Towards the poor they were neither avaricious of money, nor of affection. Often they gave up a part of their recreation to instruct them, so pitiable was their ignorance, especially of things concerning their salvation. They could be found teaching working-men their catechism, men who had never approached the Holy Table, and leading them to the communion rail for the first time. It was not enough to help the poor who came to the college door; they hunted them up in their miserable dwellings. How many attics have witnessed this touching sight! The Father who directed the band, or its appointed leader, encouraged and instructed the parents in the truths of their religion. Others catechised the children, giving them a picture as a reward and a souvenir of their visit.

Then all retired, leaving behind them greater resignation, and the Christian thought that poverty is the gold with which heaven is bought. More than two hundred families were visited in this way in a year. Both city and village were recipients of the holy charity of these pupils. Remembering always that they were the sons of Mary, they infused devotion to the Holy Virgin into the hearts which they undertook to succor, and their zeal went the length of trying to make them preachers also, thus leading misery to seek a comforter and a mother in Mary.

If the associates set an example of piety by works of charity, they were in return edified from time to time by the piety of their protégés. As Father de Bussi relates: "One day, in one of our visits, we found a poor widow whose misery was great because of the high price of bread, and who was therefore unable to get food for her numerous and half-famished family. While I was talking with her, one of her children came near our basket of provisions, devouring it with his eyes. One of the associates, observing the child's hungry look, gave him some fruit from the basket. The child took it, and, holding it in his hand, glanced towards his mother. 'You know very well what you should do,' she said, looking at the same time at the image of the Holy Virgin. The child immediately laid the fruit at Mary's feet, kneeling before her with hands clasped in prayer. Moved to tears, the visitors gave the fruit back to the child, and ever afterwards took special care of this pious family."

Such instances as these, or at least others equally edifying, were quite frequent, and were useful to our young disciples of Christian charity.

"I was a prisoner, and you visited me," our Lord will say at the Last Day, when, after taking account of the merits of the just, He is ready to give them their eternal reward. The associates could not neglect the work of visiting prisons. They might have been seen penetrating into those places where criminals expiate their crimes; among miserable beings without sense of right or wrong, some guilty only of theft or of similar delinquency; others awaiting criminal condemnation; others, again, already sentenced either to the galley or to death; the greater number embittered by punishment, and only meditating vengeance; all thinking only of their hard fate, their evil habits, their revengeful and bitter thoughts, made any effort towards their conversion exceedingly difficult. The young men went directly among them, prayed with them, taught them the rosary; the Father visitor meantime giving them a short instruction. The way to their hearts was through almsgiving. Often, at the sight of a charity specially lovely in the young, the bitterness of the men would give way. They learned to see the justice of their penalty, and encouraged each other to bear it with resignation. One of them, as he went to the scaffold, said, "It is just that he who has taken the life of a fellow-being should die, and thus satisfy divine justice." This special work was not free from sorrow and trial. More than once charity had to encounter brutal stubbornness. On the other hand, how many conversions consoled the young apostles of the Bicêtre and Conciergerie prisons! Among them one of the most remarkable was that of an old soldier, whose whole life had been passed in abject ignorance. His soul, which knew no faith, was given up to despair. One day an associate approached him, saying, "A soldier should be brave and bear his lot with more courage." Still the veteran was obdurate. Changing his tactics, the young man then told him of God and of His infinite mercies. At these words the old soldier's heart softened; he began to believe in so good a Father. With faith, hope and comfort came to him. The staff for visiting the sick was not less faithful than that which devoted itself to the poor and to prisoners. An ample field was found in the great Hôtel Dieu, where both soul and body could be delicately ministered to. As in other divisions of their sodality, temporal aid, sympathy, and religious instruction fell to the share of the young pupils. How many instances of charity and zeal, and how many happy fruits of this apostolate could be enumerated! At one time, to give the patients amusement and occupation, a library was collected; at another, retreats were given; at all times, going from bed to bed, kind words were spoken to all. As a last example, an edifying instance of generosity was that of a young man who could not see a case of suffering without the wish to relieve it. It happened that at the Hôtel Dieu there was a patient who was about to be discharged as convalescent, but who was still weak from the effects of his illness. The young visitor respectfully asked the superior why she could not keep the patient longer? "Alas!" replied the Sister, "we have no longer a free bed for him." "And how much does a bed cost?" "My child," answered the Sister, "all the money you have to give would not suffice, for a bed costs twenty francs." The generous youth took the sum from his pocket (all he had for his own little expenses), sacrificing it willingly for the good of another, and saw his protégé comfortably in his bed before he left the hospital.

Almsgiving at the homes of the poor did not

not always conveniently include spiritual help. Therefore the director of the sodality organized a work which produced much fruit. As usual he found admirable co-operators in his young people. He gathered the poor together in a chapel, where temporal relief and religious instruction were combined. Soon more than four hundred men and three hundred women frequented the chapel. The method of instruction was the same, whether at the chapel or the hospital. In order to secure attention, a controversial form was adopted. Thus the associates became instructors of the poor, imitating their Divine Master, who on the plains of Judea taught His precepts to the unfortunate and the humble. There were special exercises for retreats and for the month of Mary. More than once Divine Providence blessed the zeal of these children by remarkable conversions. At the close of one of the instructions, in which the young preacher had dwelt upon the justice of God, and called upon his hearers not to put off their conversion until the last moment, a man said to him, with deep feeling, "All those who will not be converted this very day, are already condemned." Another, after long resistance, at last renounced his evil ways, and brought five of his dissipated companions to the confessional.

If it was impossible that each member should bear an active part in all the charities undertaken by the confraternity, each at least could contribute something in the way of alms to the work of others. Sometimes the sufferings of Christ were recalled to their minds; sometimes direct appeals were made to their charity. By such considerations and by reiterated appeals, a love for suffering humanity was kept alive in their hearts. Besides regular collections, the pupils of both the junior and the senior divisions, got up sales and other enterprises by which they sought to make the college a real bureau of charity. Self-sacrifice was not unknown to them. From their earliest years they practised this great virtue, so strengthening to character, so softening to the heart.

One word will show to what point charity ruled among them: when the college was closed in 1828, the principal citizens of Amiens presented a petition to the king, in which they said: "Saint-Acheul relieves the regular charity bureaus by its generous alms; it dispenses annually at least fifty-two thousand pounds of bread to the poor," — a testimony of which the societies under Mary's patronage may well be proud. A model of charity which all should imitate who have the happiness of being brethren of these associates truly worthy of their Mother!

Our readers may have been astonished, perhaps even discouraged; they may say: "All this is no doubt admirable, but can such examples be followed in these days?" Do not misunderstand us. Zeal should be directed by prudence, and prudence must consider and weigh the actual state of things. We thought an account of the confraternities of Saint-Acheul, during the short period of 1814 to 1828, might stimulate or encourage the zeal of many other college sodalities; hence our motive in writing it. At that time the Conferences of St. Vincent de Paul were not established. Later, in the greater number of the Society's colleges, the sodalities of the Holy Virgin furnished those associations with active members. Under the presidency of their director they cultivated the habit of aiding and comforting the poor, and became experienced in that science which Holy Scripture calls a source of happiness: *"Beatus qui intelligit super egenum,"*— the science of poverty and misery.

From a report of the conference of the College of Notre Dame at Tournay, we learn that, long before the founding of the Society of St. Vincent de Paul, the practice of personally visiting the poor had been introduced there, both among the sodalists and the boarding and day pupils.

In the depth of winter the youths carried their

small alms to the poor of Frasnes and of Ellezelles; and at the time of first communion they again drew upon their own resources to furnish suitable clothes for a few poor children.

When, towards 1850, the Conferences were established in Belgium, nine pupils, all of them members of the sodality, were led to found one within the college; thus, a president, secretary, and treasurer were elected on the 9th of May, 1851. Uniting their own resources with the thousand ways in which charity delights to be generous, they raised over three thousand francs the first year. They assisted forty poor families in the suburbs. We feel constrained to resist the pleasure of naming those among the first thirty-six members of this conference, whom gratitude has since discerned in the annals of all the great Catholic charities, the greater part of them blessed names, names that have remained faithful to the inspirations of their youth.

The Conference of the College at Tournay was aggregated to the central bureau on December 7, 1852, through the influence of Baron de Gerlache. It has continued to publish its annual reports. Other educational houses founded private conferences, either by the aid of their sodalities, and more frequently by their aid alone; or they initiated the oldest of the associates in the work of the local conferences.

Many more things might be said in praise of the clients of Mary in our colleges. We might speak of their devotion to the work of instructing first communicants; of their support of free schools; of their aid to the old men in charge of the Little Sisters of the Poor. We might tell of their zeal in collecting the modest contributions of their fellow members, from week to week, in aid of the Societies of the Propagation of the Faith and of the Holy Childhood, or of the work of St. Francis de Sales. The directors of the pupils' sodalities know how much this weekly exercise of the apostolate develops the seeds of vocation. Further details would bring us directly into contemporaneous events. We think we have said enough to show that a fertile field is open to the sodalists, and that there is nothing to prevent them from imitating their predecessors, those of Saint Acheul and of Notre Dame of Tournay, as well as the first students of the Roman College, an account of whose charitable works we gave in the beginning of this history.

It is time to turn to a more interesting part of our subject. We must hasten to review the sodalities of men and of youths, with a special regard to the works of charity which they have accomplished. In this necessarily incomplete exhibit, we shall follow the chronological order, stopping only when touching too closely upon our own times.

CHAPTER IV

Sodalities of Men

IN this category, the first which claims our attention is the Paris sodality, which has already been spoken of (Book III. ch. I.). Under the wise direction of the Abbé Legris-Duval, it gave birth to a benevolent society divided into three sections: one for the hospitals, another for the prisons, and the third for the Savoyards. Each section had its president, yet every six months a general assembly was held at the headquarters of the sodality. A report was made on the general condition of the society, and on the results obtained from its three branches respectively.

The hospital work dated from the time when the Fr. Delpuits formed the nucleus of this generous union of young men. From that time on, it continued to increase. With the concurrence of the board of directors, each associate repaired on certain days of the week, and at given hours, to the men's wards which had been assigned him. There, having read aloud some suitable selection, he visited the sick who were in their beds, inciting them to accept sufferings or death in a Christian spirit.

The work among the Savoyards collected together in various quarters of Paris, on Sundays, those poor children from Auvergne and Savoy, who had come up to the great capital to find work as chimney-sweeps. Orders for bread were distributed to them after each meeting, to induce them to be punctual. Many of these poor lads prepared themselves worthily for their first communion, and carried away with them an undying recollection of that day.

The work in prisons succeeded in obtaining the separation, in common prisons, of young delinquents from older criminals. The prison authorities, yielding to the representations of the associates, consented even to a separate house for them, and confided its direction to the Brothers of the Christian Schools. These different undertakings continued to prosper under Fr. Ronsin, who in 1814 succeeded the Abbé Legris-Duval as director of the sodality. For thirteen years the most distinguished men of all ranks, and the *élite* of the young were formed, by his care, in the practice of Christian virtue. They were the most active members of the benevolent society, which admitted others who were not members of the sodality and besides, it had been thought best even to give the society a special director, the Abbé Desjardins, a former curé of the foreign missions. The revolution of 1830 stopped the activity of both societies, which until then had combined their works of piety and zeal.[1] One of the noblest recollections connected with the Paris sodality is, the work under the invocation of St. John Francis Regis. It originated in 1826 with Jules Gossin, king's counsel, a most fervent sodalist. Its object was to facilitate the civil and religious marriages of those poor who live disorderly lives, and to legitimatize their children. The Christian and moral character of this society is so well known and appreciated, that it is unnecessary to enlarge upon it. It has branches in all large Catholic towns. It was necessarily placed under the care of the secular clergy. M. Gossin, whose name is held in honor by the sodalities, was not uninfluential in originating the conferences of St. Vincent de Paul. At least we know a book of his which suggested the idea of this society, by making the generation of 1830 love the great benefactor of the poor; it is called "St. Vincent de Paul, portrayed by his Writings."[2]

[1] Guidée, Notices II., p. 68–81.
[2] Paris, Blaise, 1834, 16º, 507 pp.

Some twenty years ago, F. Carayon[1] said that the sodality had become a failure in Paris through the unpopularity of its name, which Voltairian impiety had tried to dishonor. Under a new and less compromising form, and under a new name, Catholics fearlessly re-established their work of charity. We do not pretend to say that the society of St. Vincent de Paul is a reproduction of the sodalities of the Holy Virgin; we only say that its programme of associated works of charity is a happy imitation of the work of the sodalities. The conference soon had to encounter the enemies of Catholic liberty; the enemy of the sodalities soon perceived in them the eternal object of his hatred, that is to say, practical and true Christianity. Let us say that the sodalities cheerfully rally under the banner of St. Vincent de Paul, and that, thanks to the excellent organization of the conferences, they are able to carry out more easily and more effectually, by their means, those good works which give to piety its nutriment and its consolation.

While Fr. Ronsin sustained the work of the Abbé Legris-Duval, Fr. Pierre Roger directed a sodality of Notre Dame des Victoires in a chapel of the church of St. Thomas Aquinas. This fraternity was composed of officers of the regiments of the

[1] Histoire Abrégée des Congrégations, Paris, 1863; preface.

Guard; a few generals were also admitted. Before long, unhappily, the meetings had to be discontinued; not because men were not to be found who could unite loyalty and courage with piety, nor that the exercise of that discretion which the existing state of the public mind required, gave grounds for suspicion; but, that hatred had recourse to every means for throwing discredit upon their generous efforts for the faith, and the military sodality of Paris was obliged to suspend its meetings. This happened in 1828.

It must be confessed that to undertake such works of benevolence in the face of the infidelity of that day, required the boldest confidence, or rather an unflinching courage.[1] The famous July ordinances came to prove it only too soon. The French Jesuits, sacrificed by a timid government, were obliged to break up their colleges, finding in Switzerland and elsewhere means of carrying on Christian education.

[1] Let us here recall to the honor of the young men who devoted themselves to the service of Pope Pius IX., that a sodality with the title of Mary Immaculate was formed from their ranks under the direction of Mgr. Sacré; its members, numbering about one hundred, were all Belgians, and held their meetings every fortnight. In this sodality at least, human respect did not prevent the union of piety with courage. Its members proudly wore the badge of Mary under their Zouave uniforms, and the event proved that the frank and public practice of our holy faith never weakens courage in battle, nor compromises military honor. — Précis Historiques, 1862, p. 205.

The college of Fribourg, founded by the blessed Peter Canisius, had been restored to the Society of Jesus some twelve years before this, and the French exiles not only found flourishing sodalities there among the pupils, but also among the working and middle classes.

Nothing more admirable, more edifying could be imagined — so speaks an eye-witness — than the sight which the Latin sodality offered to faith. It was composed of old students of the college, of many prominent citizens, and of ecclesiastics. Its titular feast was celebrated on the 25th of March, with a solemnity which left a deep impression on all hearts. Old sodalists assembled on that day, in the college church, from all parts of the country; magistrates, military men, and the clergy came to rekindle their zeal in this home of their early piety. A prie-dieu had been reserved for the Bishop in the choir, two others for the chief officials of Fribourg. After the sermon, which was in Latin, the vow of perpetual fidelity to Mary was renewed: lighted taper in hand, the Bishop going first, the assembly following, all made their act of consecration. This glorious homage to their Patroness ended, the sodalists laid down their tapers at the foot of Mary's throne, and, passing before their chief pastor, kissed his pastoral ring, thus declaring their loyalty to the representative of Divine Authority.

During their exile, while the French Jesuits continued to devote themselves to the cause of education, they did not wholly cease from governing the sodalities that were in France.

Not to prolong this sketch, we will only recall to mind F. Maxime de Bussi, who, after having devoted himself to the young for many years, consecrated himself to the Apostolate. The town of Puy was the principal field of his labors. Persuaded that men should place themselves at the head of a religious movement, and that it belongs to them to shield the interests of the faith by example and authority, he began, in 1835, to organize a sodality for men, choosing them from all classes of society. It numbered, almost constantly, from six to eight hundred associates. The venerable missionary made no secret to anyone of his tender affection for his well-beloved sodalities, as it pleased him to call them. He identified himself, as it were, with them, was the confidant of their sorrows and trials, their counsellor in difficulties, the assiduous and discreet minister to their necessities, the father and guardian angel of their children.

During eighteen years he refused every engagement for the last half of Lent, that he might himself give his people their retreat. His devotedness was blessed by God. Every year on the solemn Easter Day, some twelve or fourteen hundred men received Holy Communion in St. George's Church. His sodality erected a marble monument over his grave in the Chapel of St. Valerius, which recalls the memory of the good works of this pious director.

The confraternities for men and youths have nowhere been more flourishing, in this century, than in the Rhenish provinces. The whole zeal of the Jesuits of Aix-la-Chapelle, of Coblentz, of Cologne, of Düsseldorf, of Mayence, of Bonn and of Essen was concentrated upon the men's sodalities. These rendered such invaluable services to religion, that in 1865, the General Assembly of the *Katholische Vereine* spoke of them as a highly commendable institution. Those of Aix-la-Chapelle united, in six or seven different sections, persons from every class of society: prominent citizens, directors, employees of different boards of government, people of the middle class, merchants, workingmen, apprentices, students, all were helped to preserve the integrity of their faith, and trained in solid and enlightened piety. Many committees selected from among the sodalists were conspicuous for their zeal in doing good. One maintained a library for the people, another managed the Peter's Pence collections, a third organized and supported schools for adults. During the Franco-German war, special committees (*für die Charitas*) devoted themselves to the care of the wounded. Not only did they gather together necessary supplies for the relief of such unfortunates, but they spent a part of each day and night in the hospitals and ambulances.

For more than ten years since persecution drove the Jesuits from Germany, the confraternities have been kept up by the zeal of the secular clergy, in the hope that better days might enable them to strengthen and extend themselves.[1]

Perhaps we may be permitted to compare the sodalities of the Rhenish provinces with those described by the Very Rev. Fr. Anderledy in a recent letter: "I remember," writes the Vicar-General of the Society of Jesus, "having seen, in the United States of America, sodalities composed of thousands of men, who approached the Holy Table every month. In one of them, at St. Louis, young men and students numbered more than eight hundred. In Chicago, the numerous sodalities of men divide the Sundays of the month among them, in order to fulfil the rule of monthly communion. Often, on the same Sunday, at different Masses, the church of the Jesuits is

---

[1] Report of the Sodalities of Mary for men: Aix-la-Chapelle, Jacobi, 1880. The Sodalities of Mary and their importance in our time. From " Der Katholik, 1855."

filled with crowded ranks of sodalists who have come to partake of the Holy Mysteries. The cities of Boston, Baltimore, St. Louis, Cincinnati, and New York, count each about four thousand members, divided among from five to twenty different branches. There is no large city which does not offer the edifying spectacle of at least one numerous sodality for men, under the patronage of the Blessed Virgin Mary." [1]

Without counting the College sodalities, the Belgian Province of the Society of Jesus has established twenty-five sodalities of older and younger men. They number at the present time over four thousand members.

In 1835 a sodality of young men which had been inaugurated at Louvain, in the ancient Collegiate Church of St. Peter, was transferred first to the Chapel of Ease of Notre Dames des Fièvres, and lastly to the Company of Jesus. This body exerted itself always with zeal and success to promote the exercises of the Month of Mary.

The custom had already been introduced among Christian families of consecrating the month of flowers to the most Holy Virgin. To the great advantage of Christian piety, thanks to the initiative taken by the associates, as well as to the

---

[1] Woodstock letters, 1880, p. 72. Fructus Spirituales Prov. Marylandiæ; Fructus Ministerii Prov. Missourianæ.

emulation created by their example, all the churches in Louvain adopted this pious devotion.

In 1860 the Sovereign Pontiff, Pius IX., wished to show some mark of gratitude for the zeal which this sodality had displayed. Accordingly, at the request of its Director, aided by the entreaties of Mgr. Sterckx, Cardinal Archbishop of Malines,[1] in memory of the twenty-fifth anniversary of its foundation, he granted the favor of a Jubilee to the entire Deanery of Louvain. About the same time the first sodalities of the city of Ghent were established. Notwithstanding carefulness as to admissions, and strict observance of rule, they numbered in 1839 four hundred young men and two hundred and fifty fathers of families. This kind of congregation was even more successful at Turnhout, where the number of associates reached a thousand. Frequent reception of the Sacraments was one of the most consoling results of this good work. In 1848 the Dean of Ghent could estimate with satisfaction an increase of twenty thousand communions in his parish alone;

---

[1] Ob singularem devotionem erga B. V. Mariam, zelum propagandæ fidei officiorumque nostræ religionis, et exemplum omnium virtutum quibus ea (sodalitas) præfulget, etiam atque etiam Sanctitati suæ supplicamus, ut votis ejus ad majorem Dei gloriam et salutem animarum benigne annuere dignetur. — Litt. Ann. Prov. Belg. 1860, p. 22.

and he attributed this progress of piety to the fervor of the members of the sodality, whose example restored monthly communion to its place of honor.[1]

In 1842, at Brussels, the young lawyers, physicians, and university men, who were united in a sodality by F. Boone, under the protection of Our Lady of Mercy, started a conference of charity, whose statutes were approved by Cardinal Sterckx on the 9th of July of the same year. Their purpose was "to visit laboring men and the poor, to procure work and help for them, and especially to try to revive among them principles of religion, their only real support and hope."[2]

"Already," they wrote, "our little band begins to increase, but we feel the need of hastening its progress. Encouraged by the venerable head of the diocese, we have decided to publish our statutes, persuaded that our charitable aims have but to be known to the citizens of the capital, and they will come to us in large numbers, adding their efforts to ours for the success of our project."

Ordinary subscribers gave at once, or quarterly, an annual sum of eight francs. Leading subscrib-

---

[1] Litt. Ann. Prov. Belg. 1848, p. 20.
[2] Litt. Ann. Prov. Belg. S. J., 1842, p. 29. Règlement de l'Association de Charité sous le Patronage de N. D. de Miséricorde. Bruxelles, De Wageneer, 1842, 32 pp. 18mo.

ers collected ten other subscriptions. Extraordinary gifts were recorded in a special register for benefactors and patrons. Women were not admitted to the council, but shared in the work of visiting the poor.

Such was the modest origin of the first conference of St. Vincent de Paul in Belgium. After 1845 this popular charity, having been organized in Paris, was planted in Belgium, placing itself under the direction of the Central Council, with which the work of the F. Boone connected itself. About the same time some thirty students of Louvain began the foundation of that splendid sodality which has since received into its ranks the *élite* of the youth of the university. They felt that in the midst of that liberty which young students are thrown into on leaving college, the most solid piety and the most manly courage may succumb to the seductions of pleasure. It seemed, even, that a fatal influence was creeping over their *Alma Mater*. However that [1] may have been, the academic authorities were as favorably disposed as possible towards the pious undertaking. The rapid increase of the sodality, the large attendance at the fortnightly meetings, the zeal of many of the members for adult schools, the suc-

---

[1] Yseux. The sodality of the students of the University of Louvain. — Revue Catholique, 1875.

cess of the most fervent in their examinations, the splendid pilgrimages of three or four hundred sodalists to Montaigu, and especially the testimony of the rectors of the university, sufficiently attest the blessings and graces which the Holy Mary obtained for this noble congregation.

His Holiness Leo XIII., who to-day governs the Church, and who represented the Holy See as Nuncio at the Court of Brussels in 1843-4, honored the last reunion of the academic year by his presence. After Pontifical Benediction and the consecration of eleven new members, Mgr. Pecci received the council and replied most graciously[1] to the discourse of the Prefect, M. Ferdinand Lefebvre, promising, among other things, to give the Sovereign Pontiff an account of the touching sight he had witnessed. Raised to the Holy See of St. Peter, forty years later, it was to be his consolation to grant a Jubilee to the immense family of the children of Mary, on the occasion of the three hundredth anniversary of the sodalities.

"How many men have come here to learn what life is in its struggling reality, and to gain strength for the great battle for truth and Christian honor," said, in 1879, the venerable Mgr. Namèche, *Rector Magnificus*, "to gain the strength which comes

---

[1] Manuscript diary of the sodality, 18 July 1844.

from above, and to assure themselves of the sympathy of brothers who share the same convictions and who pray at the feet of the same Mother! Dispersed through every grade of society, senators, representatives, magistrates, lawyers, physicians, engineers, merchants, manufacturers, those three or four thousand men whose names may be read in the golden book of the sodality, continue still to place their faith and their religious duties above everything else; showing and proving to all, by word and example, that in the forum, as well at the domestic hearth, religious, practical faith is the one important thing for men and nations, and the only solid foundation of the state."[1]

At the time of the fiftieth anniversary of the university, Mgr. Pierærts, the honored successor of ·Mgr. Namèches, referred to the sodality of the Holy Virgin, paying merited homage to its works of zeal and faith. We subjoin an extract from his report of the 12th of March, 1884: —

"Do you not hear it said every day, gentlemen, that, in our noble and beautiful land, the university of Louvain is the bulwark of the faith? that in her there is strength, hope and salvation, because she has preserved sound doctrines, because all

[1] Address of Mgr. Namèche before the meeting of the students' sodality. . . . Louvain, Ch. Fonteyn, 1879.

her efforts tend to uphold good morals, because the young find societies in her, which I gladly call societies for mutual aid and preservation: the conferences of St. Vincent de Paul, which founded and are still sustaining so many others where the faith is preserved under the shield of charity; the sodality of the Blessed Virgin, which, though it no longer inscribes emperors and kings on its rolls, yet its ever-illustrious records show some seven hundred and eighty-four students, at the present time serving under the name and banner of Mary; the inheritor of the 'Angelic Hosts' of our ancient alma mater, the conference of St. Thomas Aquinas, proud of the distinguished circle under the protection of the holy Doctor assigned by Leo XIII. to the Catholic universities of the world as their patron; the catechetical school for adults, which presents to the gaze of heaven and earth the touching spectacle of seventy young men devoting their time of recreation, every evening, to advising and instructing the sons of working-men; neither discouraged nor fatigued at anything when it is a question of helping souls, of preventing disaster, of courageously assisting society when it is in trouble.

"Finally, gentlemen, I repeat it, there is strength, hope and salvation in the university of Louvain, because her spirit is eminently Christian and she is not afraid to announce her faith publicly; whether, preceded by the cross, her members walk in procession through the streets, chanting prayers of our liturgy, when the successor of St. Peter opens to the world the treasures and pardon of a Jubilee ; or whether, in the month of May, she organizes, with yearly increasing devotion, those splendid pilgrimages to the shrine of Our Lady of Montaigu, founded in old times by our princes, and whither our princes of to-day go, amid prayers and canticles to the edification of all Belgium, to fulfil their pious and royal vows."

We may add to this eulogy of the sodality of Louvain, that it subsequently furnished the most devoted members, who were also the first founders of the sodalities for men which at the present time are so prosperous in Brussels, Antwerp, and in other principal cities of Belgium.

We should, however, overstep the limits which we have planned for our little history, were we to describe the latest foundations. The zeal of their directors and members is an earnest of their future. Faith is strengthened, hope is revived at the sight of two or three hundred faithful servants of the Mother of God, courageously professing their religion in the face of an unbelieving public; considering it an honor and a merit to form the escort of the most Adorable Sacrament, or of the image of the ever blessed Virgin, when it is carried in peaceful triumph through the streets of the Belgian cities.

CHAPTER V

Importance of Sodalities in our Day

As we said in an earlier part of this account, men have from the beginning recognized the necessity of union; they have seen that a strength comes from the principle of association, which the individual does not possess. Neither side, either the good or evil, could afford to neglect this resource which multiplies human power and activity so greatly. Let us confess, nevertheless, that in these modern days, the enemies of Holy Church appear to have succeeded better in grouping and uniting their forces than her friends have done.

Is it because the rivalries of ambition, mutual hatred, and the quarrels of selfishness, in conflict with selfishness itself, make union necessary, a central power requisite — a governing force giving a cohesion that is external rather than real? It may be so, but harsh discipline, a rod of iron, authority which either bends or breaks; and on the other hand, selfish interests, pliant, ready for anything, are often the secret of the union of unbelievers.

Christians, so long as their conscience is not forced and they are allowed the free exercise of their religion, do not trouble themselves so much about this kind of union. United in faith and love in Holy Church, their ready and contented submission to religious and civil authority opens a certain and an honest career to them ; a career of virtue and honor under the direction of those whom our Lord constituted representatives of His divine authority. They are peaceably journeying towards the City of God. They lay no snares for anyone; they brood over no evil plots. Why, then, should they be occupied about the organization of central associations ?

In a normal condition of things, the idea would hardly have entered their minds, excepting so far as piety and zeal should find in association a precious means of bettering the condition of our Lord's suffering members, and of bringing wanderers from the faith back into the fold.

At the present time the situation is not normal. The Church everywhere is a prey to persecution, and her children share the hatred of which their Mother is the object. Peace and liberty for them are an exception. Wickedness and disorder assumed, at the beginning of our century, such power and boldness, that at last even the good seemed to have capitulated and to have delivered up the stronghold. They thought themselves happy if able to take refuge behind that weak rampart called "freedom of personal convictions."

Besides, human respect ruled Catholic consciences for a long time, keeping all public manifestation of faith in check. This has been the plague of our age in France, in Belgium, and in every place where the irreligious revolutionist has taken a quasi-official position. People dissembled that they were practical Christians. Could any true faith or zeal long tolerate such an indignity? Liberty to profess the faith in broad daylight must be regained. To this end some Catholics, like the seven thousand Israelites who did not bend the knee before Baal,[1] began the movement for the association and union of Christian strength, from which have arisen innumerable societies of every kind, living witnesses of the marvellous power of expansion of Catholicity.

As Leo XIII. recently said in his admirable encyclical, entitled "*Humanum Genus*": "Such a violent attack on the part of our enemies required a defence as vigorous in return." If violence be the characteristic of the enemies of the

[1] III. Kings xix. 18.

Church, what should be the characteristics of the defenders of the Faith? Let us learn from the Sovereign Pontiff, who says: "Let the good unite together in a vast coalition for action and prayer; let them become invincible through concord and union. *Amplissimam quamdam coeant opus est et agendi societatem et precandi."* In some Catholic countries Catholics had forestalled this appeal of the Vicar of Jesus Christ, and had already begun a serious resistance to the enemy's league. Germany was witness to the noble coalition which the "Katholische Vereine" organized against the Protestant colossus. Though weak at first, the German Catholic Union, under the direction of its pastors, has been, through enduring patience, the despair of its persecutors.

The Belgian Catholics, true to the liberty and the faith of their ancestors, have been able, thanks to their co-operation with the clergy, to reduce to impotence the audacious undertaking of a government that pretended to keep neutral; they have adhered to the principle of Christian education, and prepared a happier future for their country. The Sovereign Pontiff's encyclical will certainly arouse a movement of resistance and expansion everywhere; it will everywhere stimulate the ardor and confidence of the sons of the Catholic Church. We do not intend to speak here of those numerous political associations whose principal aim has been the furtherance of conservatism; nor of the multitude of societies for promoting letters, science, art, and all that is indirectly of interest to Christianity. We merely wish to examine the part the sodalities of the Holy Virgin are called upon to take in the religious crusade which the Vicar of Jesus Christ wishes to see organized everywhere against the enemies of the Church.

Their part, as history shows us, is a peaceful one, and differs essentially from that of circles and other associations which Catholics have established for political ends. Is it a less important one? Joseph de Maistre, the most dreaded adversary of the revolution and of irreligion, when remarking upon the great conversions of this century and the reopening of the English Parliament to Catholics, wrote: " Everything foretells a general change, a magnificent revolution, of which the one just ended (as is said) was but the terrible and indispensable precursor. To make this new revolution certain, a result to which all our prayers should tend, to strike the great enemy of the Church a final blow, what is needed? Alas, that final and most decisive of all arguments, — *Conformity of conduct with the principles we profess.* If our virtues could be cited as a proof of our faith, all the respectable enemies of that faith would not only forego their prejudices, but would also throw themselves into our arms."[1] These words, so full of truth, recall to mind the martyr, Bishop St. Cyprian, who said more concisely: "*Non magna loquimur, sed vivimus.*" The early Christians did indeed present an all-powerful argument and apology to their pagan persecutors by the spectacle of their virtues. It would be a deplorable mistake and a most bitter disappointment to imagine there can be anything more important for the furtherance of the good cause and for the prosperity of the state than the training of a truly Christian race. Men who, in the contrary sense of St. Cyprian, are more powerful in speech than they are in practical virtue, would produce nothing either solid, stable, or grand, if they were numerous in the Catholic Church. The private and public life of the *true* Christian must be in perfect accord. From this point of view, we must acknowledge that sodalities and other pious associations are of great importance to the Church, but we do not in the least mean or pretend to say that they are necessary to her.

Yes, it is a great work to form practical and zealous Christians, devoted servants of our Lord

---

[1] Letter on the secular celebration of the Protestants, 1818. Lettres et Opuscules inédits, Édition de Bruxelles, II., p. 287.

Jesus Christ. This is the special work of pious associations of all kinds; whether established for the working, middle, or higher classes, they train men to be Catholics in the true sense of the word — Catholics whose conduct will be conformed to the holy principles of their divine religion. They fit men for all the great undertakings inspired by charity and zeal. They produce men who, if called to a public life, will always be an honor to society and to the Church.

But, above all, it is the youth of our age who, in their first trial of liberty, have special need of protection, and of the strength and help to be found in active piety and charity; and that is what the sodalities supply.

Pope Pius IX., in his decree *Exponendum nuper*,[1] said: "Nothing is more pleasing to us than to see the faithful, and most especially the young men, whom impiety seeks to ensnare, enrolling themselves in those confraternities whose principal aim is to sustain and animate devotion to the Immaculate Mother of God." His Holiness Leo XIII. has lately deigned to show the deep interest he takes in the sodalities for young men. Hearing of the happy results accomplished by the fervent confraternity of the *Scaletta*, which

---

[1] Granted in 1863, on the occasion of the third centenary of the first institution of the Primaria at Rome.

numbers several hundred Roman students, His Holiness caused a letter full of encouragement and kindness to be written to its Director. The Holy Father even expressed a desire to see the chapel of this pious association enlarged, and accordingly authorized the Cardinal-Vicar to contribute to the expense of the alterations.

It is a fact of experience not requiring demonstration, that young men, and Christians in general, find strength and encouragement to piety under the protection of Mary, in the example of fellow members, and in frequent communion. St. Alphonsus of Liguori applied these words to the sodalities: "*Turris David, mille clypei pendent ex ea, omnis armatura fortium*" — "They are like the tower of David; they contain a thousand shields, the whole armor of the strong;" and he added: "Such is the reason of their fruitfulness." They provide ample means of defence against hell, and they furnish opportunities for preserving grace through the practice of piety, opportunities which are almost unattainable for seculars living outside of them.[1]

The sodalities of the Holy Virgin are essentially associations for the promotion of piety. If we have emphasized their active character, we have at least considered it as but a natural result, a

---

[1] Complete works. Paris, 1835, vol. VI., p. 416.

necessary consequence, not as being the very essence of these institutions. The first object of the confraternities is firmly to root the reign of Jesus Christ and that of His holy grace in the hearts of the faithful, and then to develop Christian life. When the blessed mother of Jesus Christ stood at the foot of the cross, and heard the words of the dying Saviour, " Woman, behold thy Son ! Son, behold thy Mother ! " it was doubtless her wish to adopt the servants of her divine Son. Moreover, on the day of his consecration, the associate is admitted into the family of the privileged children of Mary. As in this public declaration at the foot of the altar, he devotes himself to the service of the Mother of God, and accepts her for his adopted mother— *Sancta Maria, Mater Dei ac mea* — the Holy Virgin, in loving return, adopts him for the child of her heart. Thus a mutual bond of a special character is created, because of the solemnity with which the tie is cemented. In truth, the Director receives the postulant by virtue of the power confided to him by the Holy See, and in the name of Holy Church, saying : " Receive these letters patent, which declare you to be a child of Mary. For the future, manifest even more earnestly than you have done that you are really her child " — "*Accipe has patentes litteras, quibus assertus es B.*

Mariæ Virginis filius, sed tu melius moribus ac pietate te Ejusdem filium exhibe." [1]

This legal adoption, made in the name of the Vicar of Jesus Christ, confers a special title to the maternal care of the Holy Virgin. Just as St. John became the son of Christ's mother more specially than did the other apostles,[2] so the sodalist is more specially her child and the object of her care. That devout servant of Mary, dear St. Alphonsus Liguori, expresses the same opinion. "As associates, by enrolling themselves in the book of the sons of Mary," says the saint, "show their desire to become her children and eminent servants, this good mother treats them in return with distinction, and protects them in life and in death. Thus they can truly say, on entering the sodality, that they have received every blessing. 'Venerunt mihi omnia bona pariter cum illa.'"[3] The annals of the sodality quote numerous striking examples of this special protection. The same saint has also cited many similar illustrations in his admirable work on the devotion to Mary.[4]

---

[1] Historical Notices, ch. 25, on the manner of admitting sodalists, and of their reception, p. 81.

[2] Crasset, Congrégations de la T. S. Vierge, édition Carayon, p. 99.

[3] Vol. cited, p. 419.

[4] See vol. cited; Recueil d'exemples, n. 23-39.

Is it then too much to say that holiness, piety, and all Christian virtues, and the love and homage of Mary are in constant connection with one another? Is it not from this admirable Mother that Jesus Christ is born in souls, and is it not she who aids them to form in their hearts, day by day, a more perfect likeness of their Divine Model? It is she who gave strong and glorious generations of Christians to past ages. The sodality has been the privileged field for her activity in the church, a field as vast as the world; for, as we have seen, sodalities have been established all over the surface of the globe, reaping everywhere the blessings which Mary has given to the primary sodality at Rome.

In this century, wherever the Society of Jesus has been able to labor for souls, it has taken up its traditional work and ardor. Whether by its own efforts alone, or by the aid of the secular clergy, it has founded numerous sodalities.

May the Jubilee which His Holiness Leo XIII. has just granted so liberally to the Sodality of the Annunciation at Rome, and to its affiliated sodalities, arouse more and more the piety and zeal of the children of Mary!

The praise which the Sovereign Pontiff designed to bestow upon the Prima Primaria is a powerful incentive to all.

APPENDIX

Brief of His Holiness, Pope Leo XIII

Leo XIII. Pope, for Perpetual Remembrance

AMONG the prosperous sodalities which have been instituted in different parts of the world in honor of the Virgin Mary, Mother of God, the place of honor belongs without dispute to the one called the *Prima Primaria*, whose name, even, shows the pre-eminence it has gained over all others.

By virtue of the Apostolic Letter given under the Fisherman's ring, by Our predecessor of blessed memory, Gregory XIII., this confraternity was canonically established under the title of the Annunciation of the Blessed Virgin Mary. Remarkable at all times for the number of its members, enriched by the Roman Pontiffs from the treasury of indulgences, it increased so rapidly that soon, by the grace of God, it spread throughout the world, and at the present time in all countries, even in continents beyond the seas, sodalities under the same name and rule recognize their Mother.

As the three hundredth anniversary of the canonical establishment of this Primary Sodality occurs on the fifth of December of the present year, Our well-beloved son, Anthony Maria Anderledy, Vicar-General of the Society of Jesus, has besought Us to be pleased to open, for this auspicious occasion, the heavenly treasures of the church of which the Almighty has made Us the distributer. Willing to comply with this request as well as We are enabled to do in our Lord, and confiding in the mercy of Almighty God, and in the authority of the Apostles, SS. Peter and Paul, — We piously concede and grant to all regular clerks of the said Society of Jesus, and to all the sodalists who are or who shall be enrolled in the said Sodality of the Annunciation of the Virgin Mary, Mother of God, on the fifth day of the month of December, of this year, or on such other day as the directors of the different sodalities shall appoint for the celebration of this Centenary Solemnity, without postponement, however, beyond the end of the year 1885, a plenary indulgence and remission of their sins, an indulgence applicable by way of suffrage to the souls of the faithful in purgatory, — on these two conditions, viz.: first, that the sodalists shall be present five times, at the exercises which precede, during nine Consecutive days, the said solemnity; second, that, if truly penitent, and after Confession and Communion, they shall devoutly visit a chapel or church of their sodality, to pray for peace among Christian princes, for the extirpation of heresy, for the conversion of sinners, and the exaltation of Holy Church, our Mother.

And, in order that the faithful may the more readily participate in these heavenly blessings, — We grant and concede by Our Apostolic authority and by this present brief, to the respective ordinaries of the places where these sodalities exist, the faculty to depute secular or regular priests (already approved) to hear their confessions, in order that, after having carefully heard them, they may, in the tribunal of conscience only, and by imposing a salutary penance, absolve the said faithful from all their sins, crimes, and misdeeds; as well as from excommunication and other ecclesiastical censures, including the penalties attached to them, which Pius IX., of blessed memory, reserved for the Roman Pontiff, in his constitution of the 11th of October, 1869: "*Apostolicæ Sedis Moderationi.*" (We except articles 1, 7, and 10 of the excommunications *latæ sententiæ*, reserved to the Roman Pontiff by the same constitution, and

We will that these reservations be maintained in full vigor.) The priests aforesaid may also commute simple vows for some other pious work, the choice being left to their prudence and discretion.

To the said clerks of the Society of Jesus, as well as to the said members of the sodalities whom infirmity or other obstacles, of whatever kind, may prevent wholly or partially from fulfilling the appointed conditions, We concede and grant that approved confessors may commute these conditions and impose other pious works, such as their penitents may be able to perform. Notwithstanding Our rule and that of the Apostolic office, not to grant indulgences *ad instar;* and this notwithstanding other Apostolic constitutions and ordinances, or other documents, however much to the contrary they may be.

This present brief is available for this one occasion only. We will and direct that copies of this present brief, either printed or written, shall have the same authority as the original instrument, provided that they are signed by a notary public, and confirmed by the seal of a person having ecclesiastical authority.

Given at Rome, at St. Peter's, under the Fisherman's ring, the 27th of May, 1884, in the seventh year of our Pontificate.

FL. CARD. CHIGI.

Leo PP. XIII

Ad futuram rei memoriam

FRUGIFERAS inter Sodalitates, quæ in Deiparæ Virginis honorem sunt ubique terrarum institutæ, principem procul dubio locum obtinet, quæ Prima Primaria appellatur, et ipso nomine prodit quantum amplitudine ceteris antecellit. Hæc enim Congregatio per Apostolicas sub Piscatoris annulo datas litteras a Gregorio XIII Prædecessore Nostro s. m. ad invocationem Beatæ Mariæ Virginis ab Angelo Salutatæ canonice primum erecta, sodalium frequentia jugiter conspicua, indulgentiarumque thesauris per Romanos Pontifices ditata ea incrementa suscepit, ut in universum terrarum orbem sese brevi Deo favente extenderet, atque ad præsens omnibus in regionibus magno etiam terræ marisque intervallo disjunctis, filiales ejusdem nominis et instituti Congregationes reperiantur. Nunc autem cum die quinta mensis Decembris hujus vertentis anni canonicæ Congregationis ejusdem erectionis centenaria solemnitas tertia vice recurrat, dilectus filius Antonius Maria Anderledy Vicarius Generalis Societatis JESU enixas Nobis adhibuit preces, ut cœlestes ecclesiæ thesauros, quorum dispensatores Nos esse voluit

Altissimus, hac auspicatissima occasione reserare dignaremur. Nos autem piis hisce votis obsecundare, quantum in Domino possumus, volentes, de Omnipotentis Dei misericordia, ac Beatorum Petri et Pauli Apostolorum ejus auctoritate confisi, omnibus et singulis tum Clericis Regularibus ex eadem Societate JESU, tum Sodalibus dictam Sodalitatem Deiparæ Virginis ab Angelo Salutatæ inscriptis, vel pro tempore inscribendis, qui vel die quinta Decembris mensis hujus anni, vel die per singularum hujusmodi Congregationum Moderatores statuendo, non tamen ultra limites adventantis anni MDCCCLXXXV quo centenaria solemnitas celebrabitur, respectivæ Congregationis Ecclesiam, vel Sacellum vere pœnitentes et confessi, ac S. Communione refecti devote visitaverint, ibique pro Christianorum Principum concordia, hæresum extirpatione, peccatorum conversione, ac S. Matris Ecclesiæ exaltatione pias ad Deum preces effuderint, dummodo novendiali supplicationi, eidem solemnitati præmittendæ saltem quinquies adstiterint, Plenariam omnium peccatorum suorum indulgentiam et remissionem, etiam animabus Christifidelium in purgatorio detentis per modum suffragii applicabilem misericorditer in Domino concedimus, atque elargimur. Ut autem Christifideles cœlestium munerum hujusmodi facilius valeant esse participes, de Apostolica Nostra auctoritate per præsentes facultatem tribuimus, ac elargimur, ex qua respectivi locorum in quibus Congregationes supramemoratæ canonice erectæ extant Antistites aliquot Presbyteros sæculares vel regulares, ad excipiendas ipsorum sacramentales confessiones alias approbatos deputare licite valeant, qui eosdem Christifideles, eorumdem confessionibus diligenter auditis, ab omnibus quibuscumque excessibus, criminibus et casibus, nec non excommunicatione, aliisque Ecclesiasticis censuris, ac pœnis desuper inflictis, Romano Pontifici vigore Constitutionis a fe: me: Pio PP. IX quarto idus Octobris MDCCCLXIX editæ, quæ incipit *Apostolicæ Sedis Moderationi* quomodolibet reservatis, exceptis casibus sub articulo primo, septimo, ac decimo excommunicationum latæ sententiæ speciali modo Romano Pontifici reservatarum ejusdem constitutionis, pro quibus reservationem in suo plene robore manere volumus, imposita cuilibet arbitrio suo pœnitentia salutari in foro conscientiæ tantum absolvere, votaque simplicia in aliud pium opus eorum similiter arbitrio et prudentia commutare possint. Clericis vero supradictis e Societate Jesu, nec non præfatis Sodalibus aliqua corporis infirmitate, seu alio quocumque impedimento detentis, qui supra expressa, vel eorum aliqua præstare nequiverint, ut illa Confessarii jam approbati in alia pietatis opera commutare possint, eaque injungere, quæ ipsi pœnitentes efficere valeant pariter concedimus, et indulgemus. Non obstantibus nostra, ac Cancellariæ Apostolicæ regula de non concedendis indulgentiis ad instar, aliisque Constitutionibus, et Ordinationibus Apostolicis, ceterisque contrariis quibuscumque. Præsentibus hac vice tantum valituris. Volumus autem ut præsentium litterarum trasumptis, seu exemplis, etiam impressis, manu alicujus Notarii publici subscriptis, et sigillo personæ in ecclesiastica dignitate constitutæ præmunitis, eadem prorsus adhibeatur fides, quæ adhibetur ipsis præsentibus, si forent exhibitæ vel ostensæ. Datum Romæ apud S. Petrum sub annulo Piscatoris die XXVII Maii MDCCCLXXXIV Pontificatus Nostri Anno Septimo.

FL. CARD. CHISIUS.

L. ✠ S.

Concordat cum exemplo, quod munitum est Summi Pontificis sigillo.
ANTONIUS M. ANDERLEDY, S. J.

Concordat cum exemplari Fesulano.

www.ingramcontent.com/pod-product-compliance
Lightning Source LLC
Chambersburg PA
CBHW020809230426
43666CB00007B/935